An Adopted Angel in Disguise

An Adopted Angel in Disguise

Information compiled by Barbara Malan

Alive Book Publishing

An Adopted Angel in Disguise
Copyright © 2025 by Barbara Malan

Dedicated to The Girls

All rights reserved. No part of this book may be reproduced or transmitted in any form or by any means without written permission from the publisher and author.

Additional copies may be ordered from the publisher for educational, business, promotional or premium use. For information, contact ALIVE Book Publishing at: alivebookpublishing.com, or call (925) 837-7303.

Book Design by Alex Johnson

ISBN 13
978-1-63132-254-9

Library of Congress Control Number: 2025911493
Library of Congress Cataloging-in-Publication Data is available upon request.

First Edition

Published in the United States of America by ALIVE Book Publishing
an imprint of Advanced Publishing LLC
3200 A Danville Blvd., Suite 204, Alamo, California 94507
alivebookpublishing.com

PRINTED IN THE UNITED STATES OF AMERICA

10 9 8 7 6 5 4 3 2 1

An Adopted Angel in Disguise

An inspirational story and tribute to a talented, spiritual and exceptional mind

1. The "adoption story" for the introduction written by Jim's parents

2. Five binders including photos, stories, school papers, poems and songs. The sequence of his life from primary years to his 12th grade, written and experienced by Jim. All material was discovered by Jim's family shortly after 1980 in his possessions. He stored his life's journey for us?

3. A list of performances by Jim over the years, pictures early and up to 1980 as Jim ages

4. Pat's book (pages 1-39) written about Jim's life. She was his teacher and school secretary at St. Isidore's grade school (1st-8th). She knew him well and followed his growing years in high school. Schools were much smaller in class size. Teachers knew all their students.

5. Pat's submission to the Oakland Diocese regarding Mother Seton's award for a student's achievements

6. Remembrances—written by Jim's mother, of his last days

Our Adoption Story

By John and Barbara Malan

July 1962 will forever be etched in our memories. James Malan, our three month old baby, was placed in our arms. In wonderment we stared at this perfect little baby. "An Angel in Disguise"

John and Barbara were married on July 18, 1959 in Haddonfield, New Jersey. So long ago! John was 29 and Barbara just turned 24. We both were born and raised in the local towns. Our first home was a beautiful brick 4-plex. Our large families all lived locally. We were such a happy newlywed couple and so in love!

John was employed by a local corporation after serving 4 years in the service. Prior service was in his college years.

Barbara began a new exciting position as a RN assistant to a very famous doctor in the Camden area. She was previously employed by other hospitals, one being the local Camden hospital, "Our Lady of Lourdes." While being employed by this hospital she became acquainted with the doctor. He was the chief OB-GYN and infertility specialist in Lourdes. He was researching for an office nurse. His prior nurse was transferred to another city. Barbara was interviewed for the position and was offered the job. The timing was perfect, as she was not working when she and John married. The offer was too good to turn down and she accepted.

Our new-married life was so filled with love and enjoyment. We were both so happy! There was so much to thank God for. We wanted to start a family. John even brought home a beautiful Siamese kitten. We both loved "Mimi," as she was our baby! She brought a great deal of happiness to our family over the years.

Barbara remembers so well visiting "Lourdes Chapel" prior to the start of each workday. The doctors' offices were two blocks past the hospital. She prayed and asked God to fulfill their dreams of becoming parents. Barbara remembers purchasing a great amount of baby clothes, blankets, accessories, etc. over their first few years of marriage. She never shared her "hoarding" with John. One beautiful day, and an emotional day it was, Barbara displayed their baby possessions to John.

During the first two years of our married life we investigated why there was no pregnancy. We researched medical, surgical and professional areas, especially consulted with Barbara's "boss" doctor. In the end the prognosis was no in our favor. It was a while before we both adapted to this sad news.

John and Barbara never thought about adoption. We prayed and discussed this new idea of becoming parents. We decided it was what we both wanted to pursue. We wanted to share our love with a baby who could be denied the joy of a family unity. We were both so excited and committed.

We shared our ideas and process of adoption with our families. They were so supportive and happy for us. John's sister had a close friend who was a social worker with Camden Catholic Charities. We met with her for a consultation. It proved to be a bleak and disappointing timeframe. She informed us that a placement would be at least two years if not longer.

Private adoption was suggested to us. Risk was involved before and after an official adoption. We both did not consider this route.

Our parish pastor was a close friend of our families. He was officially involved with Catholic Charities. We consulted with him for advice, but he was not very encouraging. There were hardly enough babies for all the applications on file at this time. He told us what the social worker had said.

Barbara remembers when her family was transferred to Scranton, PA. They resided in the Greenrich area of Scranton. She was eight years old and enrolled in Marywood Seminary, where she learned to play the piano very well. She had a special school friend named Mary. The girls played at Mary's home after school with their parents' approval. Her home was not too far from a secluded compound comprised of three very large stone buildings. These buildings were surrounded by heavy and high cyclone fencing. One hospital was for special needs children. The second was an orphanage and the third was St. Joseph's Children's and Maternity Hospital. The girls would play and communicate with these children through the fencing.

Barbara remembers her young years so vividly. They were very happy years with her loving family. They returned to Haddonfield where they resumed their lives. Barbara was 17 and completed her senior year.

1962

Barbara told Jack about her experiences as a young girl and the maternity hospital complex. Maybe they had children or infants for adoption? Especially shorter than 2-plus years.

John immediately contacted the Director. Her name was Miss McCandless and she listened to his story. She sent a very large application package. They wanted to know our history, why we wanted a baby and many other questions. We completed our "book" and returned it as soon as possible.

There were three following appointments in Scranton with her staff. This was all so new and exciting for us! We were finally contacted by the hospital that there were many similarities between us and an infant. This baby boy was 3 months old and in the process of being placed with another family. They all agreed we were the couple for that baby. Apparently our Irish heritage was very important. This baby's mother and father were both very Irish. We were informed of some history. This baby's mother was a nurse and the father was a doctor. She played the piano as well. The mother was very much involved with his placement and visited with him during his stay. His "adopted" family had to be approved by her and we were!

St. Joseph's contacted us that we were to become this special baby's parents. Our excitement was hard to contain, as well as our families.

In July, the transition was to take place in the hospital's chapel's altar. John and I were very much prepared. We previously presented his new clothes to the nurses – extras if they did not fit! We remember the first time we saw Jim was when he was blessed and baptized on the altar. We will never forget the beautiful moment when he was placed in our arms. The attending priest, Miss McCandless and staff were all so happy for us and Jim. We all prepared for this special trip to Jim's home. The hospital personnel told us earlier that Jim resembled John so much.

John and Barbara remember the car ride back to their home so vividly. Barbara even remembers the orange summer dress she wore for this special day. Jim was placed in the new tan car carrier bed on his tummy in the back seat sleeping. He was so beautiful! When he awoke we looked back and can still see him lifting his head to look around. Stopping the car and cuddling him we continued home.

Our families were anxiously awaiting his arrival. They could not believe how much he resembled John.

We will never forget this beautiful gift given to us by God. What a beautiful and blessed day for us all.

In the meantime, we shared the information with our pastor. He was very much interested in contacting St. Joseph's Hospital. Father made several trips to and from Scranton. He was informed that there were nineteen babies waiting to be adopted. There were approvals, releases, etc. by both dioceses before they were transferred to Camden Catholic Charities. The babies were all shortly placed with families.

We felt we extended our beautiful experience through God's gift to us.

We became friends with some of these happy families through the years as our children grew.

John contacted Camden Catholic Charities to place an application for another baby. He told me that I was pregnant, as he surprised me! We both wanted another baby.

Our daughter Diane was just two weeks old. Jim was two years old and happy to have a baby sister. We had another blessing. When Diane was 2 and Jim 4, John applied for another baby!

Our third child, Linda, was one week old when she was placed with us. What a happy family with our three beautiful children. When our children were 5, 3 and 1½, we were transferred to the San Francisco Bay Area (1968). We had wonderful happy years raising our children in the San Ramon Valley.

Needless to say, our families missed us, and especially their grandchildren.

This is the story of how we became the blessed, loving and proud parents during Jim's 18 years on earth. We are so grateful.

Blessings from God,

John and Barbara

Binder #1

Elementary 1968 to 1975

(First page was the image of "Jimmy's hand, 1968")

1970 to 1971

June 30, 1971

Sunday 9:30 AM

Dear Mommy, Diane, Linda and Dad,

How are things in California? Things are fine here in New Jersey.

NaNa is going to take Mrs. Lodge and Tommy and me to Radio City and to the Planetarium.

We are going to have lots of fun.

The first night dinner was rice and the second dinner was barbecued Hot Dogs and Hamburgers.

I went to Nancy McCarthy's swim meet. She got four ribbons. One came in first place, backstroke second place, freestyle third place butterfly and fourth place swan dive.

I saw Debbie and Dana and Mr. and Mrs. Simpson too.

Debbie and Dana were on Downs Farms team and Nancy was on Barclay Farms team.

Barclay Farm at the score 208 to 179.

Love,

Jimmy, NaNa and PopPop

XXX

OOO

P.S. NaNa asked me why I put Daddy's name last and I said 'cause he's a boy. (Jim was 8 years old)

Dear NaNa and PopPop

I can't wait till you come out to see me. I have so much to tell you. I love you and I hope you love me to.

Love Jimmy,

1970

* * *

June 28, 1970

Sunday 9:30 PM

Dear Mommy, Daddy and Linda, and Diane,

How is the family back there? When I landed in Pennsylvania the temperature was 72 but when I got to NaNa's house it was 63. When we were above Chicago we started to go down. When we got above Ohio we were 300 feet from the ground. Then we went over the Atlantic Ocean at 140 feet from the ground and then turned around to head west and landed in Pennsylvania. When we were 250 feet off the ground we were cloud level and you couldn't see a thing. There were two other brothers on the plane that were alone too. You should have seen the food they served on the plane. We almost landed in New York. Well I'll tell you the rest when I come home.

Love

Jimmy

(8 years old)

***

1970 (8 years old)

Dear NaNa and PopPop,

I wrote this letter when you left from here. Hope you had a nice flight home.

How are you? OK!

Before I forget, thank you for the 5 dollar you sent Diane Linda and me

Love,

Diane, Linda and Me

***

The Christmas Story

Act I

The Angel came to Mary

It was a cold morning when Mary (P _ _ _ _ _ _) heard somebody calling her name. It was an angel (M _ _ _ _ _) of God. The angel said to Mary, "Will you be the mother of Jesus (T _ _ _ _ _)?

"Oh yes, I shall be very, very happy to do what God asks of me."

"Oh, you are so kind," said the angel "and I also want to tell you that your cousin Elizabeth is also having a baby. I shall visit her. Mary ran and told Joseph (M _ _ _ _ _). When Joseph heard this he was filled with joy. He said, "When are you going to have him?" Mary said the angel did not say. Then Mary started out to see Elizabeth. After about 3 months John was born. Mary said goodbye and good luck.

Act II

Jesus is born

Mary returned. Joseph said, "How was your trip?

Mary said Elizabeth had a baby and named it John. Three weeks later they started on their journey to Bethlehem. It was many miles. They stopped at about 16 places, but nobody had any room until the 17th place. He said the only place he had was a stable down about ½ mile. Mary said, "Oh thank you very much" So they started down the road. Finally they reached the stable. There was a beautiful light. Mary said, "This is the moment we have been waiting for."

They both fell to him and said Thank you God.

(The song Joy to the World)

Act III (Final scene)

The Kings

There was a beautiful star above the stable. When the shepherds saw the star they were frightened. But an angel said FEAR NOT! Follow the star and where the star ends you shall see the King of Kings.

(Oh Come all the Faithful)

3 kings saw the star too. They wanted to follow it. Soon they got there. One of the shepherds that wasn't there when the angel said (song What Child is this). The angel said this is Jesus Christ the King of Kings. Everybody that was there praised God. This was the first Christmas.

By James Malan

3rd grade 11/'70

N _ _ _, Angel

P _ _ _, Mary

M _ _ _, Joseph

T _ _ _, Jesus

3 kings, J_ _ _, R _ _ _, P _ _ _

5 shepherds, P _ _ _, D _ _ _

The songs are

Joy to the world

Oh come all the faithful

What child is this?

May I please play the ORGAN?

***

1971 to 1972

Post Card

Dear Mommy and Daddy,

This card is from the Franklin Institute. This is the 2nd space craft, the Gemini. We took Tommy and Mrs. Lodge to dinner.

***

Feb 5, 1971

Adventure to Fra Mauro

"The Flight of Apollo XIV"

Jan 30, 1971 the three astronauts which were Alan B. Shepard, Jr., Edgar D. Mitchell and Stuart A. Roosa were taken to the elevator that would take them to the command module. They were in their seats when the countdown started. When the countdown was 12:06 there were clouds over the launch pad. The weather man said that they would have to hold the countdown at 8:02. It was a 40 minute delay. The weather men said if the rocket was not launched in 4 hours they would have to wait till March, because the sun wouldn't be at the correct angle. Alan Shepard was the first American man in space, 10 years ago (1961). Because of an ear injury they said that it was the end of Shepard's career. But he paid for a operation and his problem was solved. The Saturn 5 is 350 feet long. Now all 4 seconds in the countdown 3, 2, 1, Liftoff. 13,000 tons of fuel and thrust. In 2½ minutes the first stage burned out, the second stage fired with 6,000 miles per hour. 9 minutes after liftoff the second stage burned out. The third stage fired with 14,000 miles per hour. 11 to 12 minutes after liftoff third stage shuts off.

The rocket was going 17,500 miles per hour. The astronauts were casting in the space rocket. About 1½ hours after liftoff the third stage fired on a lunar trajectory. 6 minutes after that the third stage burned out. The doors opened up and out came the lunar module. The service module went out 180 feet, turned and tried to dock with the lunar module. But they had trouble. The two modules would not dock. It took 5 attempts to try to get them together. But they could not until the sixth attempt. They got both of them together. Then they checked out all the systems and they were off to the moon. It took them 13 hours in zero gravity. The 13 hours flew by pretty fast. They were in lunar orbit around the moon. At 12:51 AM the service module and the lunar module separated. The lunar module went twice around the moon. At 1:27 AM the lunar module landed. It was not a pinpoint landing. The lunar module landed sixty feet from the crater "Fra Mauro." 6 hours after landing the hatch opened. Down came Shepard.

Shepard's very first words as he stepped in the lunar dust were "It's been a long way but we're here." 10 minutes later Mitchell came down. He said to Shepard that he saw the service module up ahead. They got the experiments out and went to work. The moon walk lasted 3½ hours. After that they went back up the stairs to prepare for the second moon walk which would be in 7 hours. At 10:00 PM they came down the stairs again. Shepard wanted to play a joke, so he took a golf club and golf ball and hit it. They said that the ball went more than 250 miles. After 6 minutes they started to "cone crater." They were going to find some rocks that were over 400 years old. But they did not make it because the oxygen was low so they had to come back an hour earlier. The moon walk ended at 6:53 AM. So they went back into the Lunar, took a 3½ hour rest, at breakfast and prepared for lunar liftoff which would be at 10:47 AM. The countdown went fast, it was at 5, 4, 3, 2, 1 up went the lunar module. In 10 seconds it changed course so it could orbit. The orbit took 45 minutes. Then it was docking time. If the two would not dock Shepard and Mitchell would walk through space. But it was a great docking at 12:29 PM. Shepard and Mitchell had to transfer 108 pounds of moon samples. At 12:44 Shepard and Mitchell rejoined Roosa in the Kitty Hawk. At 2:46 PM the Kitty Hawk jettisoned "Antares." At 4:43 Antares crashed onto the lunar surface. At 5:27 Kitty Hawk fired to take them back to earth.

If everything goes well, the splash down will be at 4:04 PM in the central Pacific 56 miles from Hawaii.

By James Malan

Grade 4, 9 years old, 1971

***

Dear Mr. Nixon (President)   November 5, 1972 4:30 PM

My name is Jimmy Malan. I go to St. Isidore's School. In most schools you have one teacher. But, not in this school, in this school our class has 5 teachers. Their names are, Mr. S (our home room teacher), Sister E, 5th grade teacher (who teaches us math), Sister N (who teaches us social studies and is the sixth grade teacher), Sister R (who is the 7th grade teacher and teaches us singing) and the Principal of the school is Sister J (who is the 8th grade teacher and teaches us spelling). Mrs. D is in our class as a lady teacher, while Sister N and Mr. S were teaching us about the sights of Washington D.C. Sister J rushed in and showed us the letter you sent Mrs. D. All 3 of them agreed that if that ever happened to them they would surely faint. So, if you have the time would you please write a letter to Mr. S, Sister R, Sister J and Sister N? I have heard very much about you and when I saw your picture in the newspaper for the first time, I cut it out and saved it. I have been after my mom for a long time now but we just never got around to it. She says I'll get it for my birthday. But that's not until April 27th.

Jim Malan, 9 years old

***

1972 to 1973

Thur. Dec. 18, 1972

Dear you Guys,

Yesterday we went to New York. PopPop dropped us off at the United Nations Building. After we got out, NaNa realized that she had PopPop's money in her hand and he didn't have a cent. We didn't know what to do. We got in a cab and started chasing his. Soon out of sight he was. The taxi man was nice and kept telling us that everything would be alright. We turned a corner and there was PopPop a few cars in front of his. We chased him for 5 minutes, dodging traffic lights. There was much traffic. He finally had a red light. NaNa and I jumped out, ran through the traffic and caught him just in time. He was shocked. We ran back to the cab and went back to the U.N. We spent hours there. We went into the Assembly room and saw the last General Assembly of the year. We took a tour through the whole U.N. I got a solid bronze coin and some literature. We ate lunch in the cafeteria. Then we got a cab to the Empire State Building. The weather was good and we could see up to 80 miles. Then we walked from 34th street all the way up 5th avenue to 50th street. We stopped at B. Altman Lord and Taylor Sachs 5th Ave. We went to Rockefeller Center to see the ice-skaters. Then we went to St. Patrick's Cathedral and then to the top of the sixes where we met PopPop for dinner. The cheapest thing on the menu was $7.50. I got broiled steak with a salad, grapefruit, tomato juice, ice cream or souffle and Shirley Temple. We had a window seat looking down at 5th Ave. Earlier this week we went to the Smithville Inn where we saw Terry. Mr. Kraus called and I am going there tomorrow. The organ just came. It is snowing lightly. Send out some Phisohex!!! Keep this letter. Can't wait to see you.

Love

Jim,

NaNa,

PopPop

Merry Christmas

***

1973 to 1974

James Malan, Jan. 17, 1973

Air Transport

The first commercial transport started on Jan. 1, 1914. The aircraft flew 22 miles. Airlines took passengers for 5 to 10 mile rides until 2 years after the first flight was made. Then they set up little buildings that people waited in for their plane rides. Some men started a schedule of flights and posted it in the paper. Up until this time passengers were riding free, but some of the pilots started charging admission to fly. The first known admission was 5 cents a mile. Then every 2 years it went up 1-5 cents.

The first nonstop commercial flight was made on June 14, 1919. This flight went from Newfoundland to Ireland.

The U.S. has 7 major airlines: American Airlines, Braniff Airways, Delta Airlines, Eastern Airlines, Pan American World Airways, Trans World Airlines, and United Airlines. Many other countries have many other airlines.

Different Types of Airlines . . .

2 engines

DC9 – This aircraft flies short flights from 100-500 miles. Holds 100-150.

3 engines

727 – Flies short to medium flights from 500-1000. Holds 200-225.

DC10 – Flies long range, Holds 200-300. Flies 2500-3200.

<u>4 engines</u>

All of the following fly long range from 2500-3200. Hold 200-400.

880 Convair, DC8, 747, DC8 Super 10, 720

Planes of the Future

The planes of the future will be the SST and the Concorde. The SST is scheduled to start commercial in late 1974. The Concorde will fly in late 1975.

***

James Malan, Jan. 29, 1973

THE SHINY TRAIN

One day in 1959 almost the whole town of Denver was gathered around the new railroad tracks that had started at Dallas and came all the way through the Rock Mountains, through Denver and all the way to Portland. The people were waiting to see the very first train that came through their city. Soon they saw it coming. Everybody started to cheer. It was white with gold trim and the wheels rolled <u>smoothly</u> along. The engineer was a fat, jolly man who was nice and kind. Every day he would give the children a ride from one end of the city to the other. One day in 1961 he was transferred to Dallas and was to give people rides in that city. All the children were sad and didn't want him to go. But the engineer said, "I'll be back some day and we will have fun again." He wasn't even <u>proud</u> of his own train. It was black all over and it went so <u>fast</u> that everybody was afraid to even set foot on it. Soon the man didn't want to be an engineer in the city so he moved on to another one. The people were without a train. In May of 1962 a train was seen coming around the bend. It was white with gold trim just like the first one. Suddenly the people realized it was the old engineer. Everybody ran to meet him and all the children piled in to have a ride. They were so glad to have him back. He kept on giving rides until the spring of 1966 when he retired. But all through the years the people passed on the story, and it went all around the country. People still tell it today. And they will always keep on telling it so everyone will know about the kind engineer with the shiny train.

***

Spring is Here

    Spring is here,

Spring is there,

Spring is around,

I think, somewhere.

All of the birds,

Are up in the trees.

And all of the dogs

Are scratching their fleas.

And as I look down,

Upon the green ground,

I see pretty flowers,

Pink, yellow and brown.

And all this is because,

Springtime is here.

And everyone is happy,

Giving a cheer.

Where is Spring?

Come and see.

Spring is here,

Where it should be.

James Malan, Spring 1973

***

James Malan, Sept. 11, 1973

Social Studies

The Comparison of Modern America & Modern Russia

TRANSPORTATION:

America and Russia's main transportation is by air. Russia was the first to invent the Wire Braced Biplane, the Tailless Airplane, the Canard, and now the SST or the Super Sonic Transport. America was the first to invent the Concord which will be a commercial airplane by 1975-76. Russia only has one main airline, Aeroflot or Soviet Airlines. America has seven main airlines: American Airlines, Braniff Airways, Delta Airlines, Eastern Airlines, Pan American World Airways, Trans World Airlines, and United Airlines. Each of them is privately owned.

America's main aircraft is the 707 with 4 engines, the 4-engined DC8, the 2-engined 737, the 3-engined 727, and the 4-engined 747s. Russia's main aircraft in the 2-engined Caravelle Super B, the 2-engined Hawker Siddeley Comet 4C, the 3-engined Hawker Sidley Trident, and the 4-engined Ilyushin 62.

Russia's newest airplane is a fighter plane, a 4-engined RA-5C that has a cruising speed of 1200 mph. America's newest airplane is the MB-3, a 6-engined aircraft with a cruising speed of 1950 mph.

SPORTS:

Russia's main sports are swimming, track and field and gymnastics. Their best events are the 50 meters, 100 meters, and 150 meters freestyle, the 100 meters breaststroke, the 300, 350, 375 and 450 meters butterfly, the 110 meters backstroke, and the 200, 800, 1600 meters individual medley. Their star swimmers are Fredrick Azar and Jonathon Zyinkoff.

In track and field their only good races are the 100 meters, the pole vault, and the high jump.

In gymnastics they are a very strong team. Their best events are the uneven parallel bars, the high bar, and the floor exercises. Their star athletes are Albert Azaryan and Olga Korbut.

In swimming, America was the strongest team there is. Their best strokes are the 50, 100, 200, 300 400, 600, 1000, 1500, and 165 meters freestyle. The 100, 250, and 800 meter breast stroke, the 400 and 410 meters backstroke, the 100, 200, 250, 400 meters butterfly, the 200 i.m. and the medley and freestyle relays. Our star swimmers are Johnny Weissmuller, Dawn Fraser, Don Schollander, and Mark Spitz.

America is the third best team in gymnastics with people like Kathy Rigby. Our best events are the floor exercises and the vault. America is the strongest team in track and field. Our best events are the 50, 100, 200, 350, 500, 750, 1000, 1650, 2000, 3000, 5000, 5850, 7000, and the 10000 meters in track. And in the field events our best are high and low jump, discus, javelin, shot, and the pole vault.

ASTRONOMY:

In the beginning of space exploration, Russia was the first to launch a rocket, the first with the satellite, the first to put a manmade object around the sun and the moon, the first to send a manmade object to hit the moon, and the first to set a roving vehicle on the moon with a capsule that brought back samples.

America was the first to dock in space, the first to set a movie camera on the moon, the first to make a soft landing on the moon, the first to put man on the moon, the first man to drive a vehicle on the moon, the first to send a manmade object to Mars and the first to have a successful space station.

In 1977 America and Russia are going to dock with each other in space, trade spacecrafts and reenter.

In 1979 America will start the space shuttle series which will let man use a spacecraft like he would an airplane. And in the late 1990s man has drawn out plans that will get a man to Mars and return him safely to the Earth.

> Teacher's note: A very good and very complete job. I enjoyed your oral presentation very much, too. I will be glad to re-type your paper, too, if you like, very sorry about the "spill."

***

James Malan, Nov. 30, 1973

Science Project

The Planets

EARTH - Earth is 7900 miles in diameter, Avg 93 million miles from sun, one orbit 365¼ days, 24 hrs one rotation. 1 moon, 2100 miles diameter, 239,000 miles away. Temp. as low as -127, high +136

MERCURY - Nearest to sun, 2900 mls diameter, 88 days for orbit. 58½ days one rotation. No atmosphere. No moons. Low -10, high 200+. 36 million mls from sun.

VENUS - 7600 mls diameter. 67 million mls from sun. 7½ mons 1 orbit. 8 mons 1 rotation. Thick clouds,

MARS - 4200 mls diameter. 142 million mls from sun. 1 rotation 24½ hrs. 1 orbit 23 mons. 2 moons. High temp. 80+ low -110.

JUPITER - Largest planet. 86,000 mls diameter. 483 million mls from sun. 12 yrs 1 orbit. 9½ hrs rotation. 12 moons. High temp. -200, low -450.

SATURN - 2nd largest planet. 71,500 mls diameter. 886 million mls from sun. 1 orbit 29½ yrs. 1 rotation 10½ hrs. 10 moons. High temp -200 low -500. Flat rings. Small rocks, dust.

URANUS - 29, 200 mls diameter. 1,783,000,000 mls from sun. Orbit 84 yrs. Rotation 11 hrs. 5 moons. High temp -250 low -600.

NEPTUNE - 28,000 mls diameter. 3 billion mls from sun. Rot 16 hrs. High temp -380 low -750.

PLUTO - Farthest from sun. 5000 mls diameter. Crooked orbit. Orbit 248 yrs. Rotation 6½ dys. High temp -350 low -900.

***

1974 to 1975

LOOK ALL AROUND

LOOK AT THE PLANTS,

LOOK AT THE TREES,

LOOK AT THE GRASS,

IT'S UP TO MY KNEES.

LOOK AT THE DOGS,

ROMP IN THE LAKE,

LOOK AT THE FAWN,

CALLING HER MATE.

LOOK AT THE BIRDS,

DOING THEIR THING,

BUILDING THEIR NESTS,

HOW SWEETLY THEY SING.

AND ALL THAT YOU SEE,

IS WHAT GOD MADE TO BE,

LOOK AT THE ANIMALS,

WILD AND FREE.

LOOK AT THE SKY,

LOOK AT THE GROUND,

LOOK AT THE BROOK,

LOOK ALL AROUND.

Jim Malan

1974 (12 yrs old)

***

January 2, '74

Dear Mom and Dad,

This is the Christmas card NaNa found while she was doing some bills. She had it all made up and forgot to send it. I'm still working on her to go to Florida. Next week we are going to see the Gordons. Today I got all of my camera equipment—film, electronic flash, case.

Love,

Jim

***

Jim Malan, March 1, 1974

Social Studies Report

Ancient Civilizations

MESOPOTAMIAN CIVILIZATION:

The Mesopotamian beginnings are best known to us. Many excavated sites of ancient settlement show the transition from very early times to full civilization. For half a million years the inhabitants of what is now Iraq were food collectors living in very small groups. A site in the Kurdish hills, going to about 6000 B.C., suggests a larger settlement, out of caves in the open, and provided with domesticable if not yet domesticated—sheep, goats and pigs. In this part of the world we still need more evidence for settlements and supplementing wild food by care of those wild grasses which became the first cereals of agriculture. But in sites in Palestine have been found sickle-like tools made with flint and used to cut some grass—possibly undomesticated barley and emmer. The first food producing villages lie not in the swampy southern river valleys but on the grassy hill country of the Fertile Crescent. By about 5000 B.C. people were living in clusters of mud houses, growing wheat, barley, and peas and provided with domestic sheep and goats. Not long after 4000 B.C. an expansion took place into riverine southern Mesopotamia; the villages grew into temple-towns with markets; by 3500 B.C. large and monumental public buildings, clay tablets showing first notations, for keeping accounts, and—somewhere more speculatively to be asserted—a city-state democratic but giving powers and perhaps control of an irrigation system to a "king" in emergencies—all recognize the arrival of the first civilization.

This "Sumeric" civilization produced states later conquered by Semitic peoples; the empire of Hammurabi fell and, in Toynbee's view, the civilization itself gave rise to the closely related "Babylonic!" Of all the ancient civilizations, this one most influenced our own. While the transmission of their inventions to the Hellenic culture and then to modern peoples cannot always be demonstrated, the Mesopotamians were the first to have important elements of knowledge that underlie Western, and in part, other civilizations such as: writing, contracts, accounts, law codes, weights and measures, money (not coined), and the elements of astronomy and mathematics.

EGYPTIAN CIVILZATION:

In Egypt, in the Faiyum, and along the Nile Delta, village life was established a little later than in Mesopotamia—in 5000 B.C. In 4000 B.C., appeared elements known earlier to the Mesopotamians: cylinder seals, the potter's wheel, and writing. The occupation of the Nile Valley was begun, swamps drained, and irrigation works undertaken. Settlements arose all along the valley; these were eventually united in one state; but in spite of great advances in technology and social and political institutions they were but temple-towns. In 2000 B.C. A CIVILIZATION OF GREAT MEANING AROSE WITHOUT WHAT WE KNOW AS URBISM. The Egyptian civilization was self-contained and long enduring; it showed its greatest vitality early, then declined into formalism, leaving civilization for their ancestors to carry on.

INDIAN CIVILIZATION:

The Indian civilization is known to us from sites excavated in the Indus Valley, and from lesser evidence elsewhere from Baluchistan to Kathiawar, is a civilization closely connected as to food stuffs, material, and many other detailed forms of artifact with civilization of the ancient Mediterranean. But by 4000 B.C., it already showed elements characteristic to later India: a Siva-like figure, phallic stones, and an Indian type of bullock cart. It is certain that a great and powerful civilization started the same time as the Mediterranean. This civilization kept up without falling for several thousand years, and conquered many other civilizations.

CHINESE CIVILIZATION:

It has a system of writing, it had business, people working for other people and people working for themselves, and they had respect for their religion. They were very holy people and would do anything for their gods. They had gods like, the god of rain, the god of sun, the god of the sea, the god of death, the god of eternal life, and many, many others. The Chinese were invaded a lot and they were afraid that they might be conquered so they built a very great wall called The Great Wall of China. This wall was many hundreds of miles long and took years to build. In some places the wall was 8 feet thick and 10 to 12 feet tall. This did keep out the enemies who tried to attack China.

BIBLIOGRAPHY:

Collier's Encyclopedia, Vol. 3 Pages 409-412

World Book Encyclopedia Vol. 5 Pages 8-203

***

What I think of Mr. Nixon resigning

I don't know about Watergate and all this of confusion going on in America today. A lot of people are glad to see him resign and a lot of people are not. Some people have said he has committed some crimes. Maybe he has, but he has also made friends with China, Russia, and other countries. Some people say that while he was trying to make friends with other countries, his colleagues got him in to this Watergate forcing him to resign.

Jim Malan

12 years old

August 8, 1974

6:25 P.M.

***

November 6, 1974 (Jim 12 yrs. old)

Mr. and Mrs. Malan

Sister Joan

I did want you to know how very pleased we are with Jim and his participation at Mass. He played the organ very well at our last First Friday Mass.

Sister Joan Griffin

***

1975 to end!

James R. Malan

2629 Trotter Way

Walnut Creek, California 94598

Sat. Feb. 1, 1975

Dear NaNa & PopPop,

I want to thank you so much for the fabulous trip that you made possible for me to have. I am looking forward to our cross-country trip this summer. We are all real excited because as you know, we are looking for a brand new station wagon. We have already gone to some car places and have gotten some bids. We are going to get it before the end of March for we will probably end up ordering one. We are going to get a lot of options and Dad will get an executive price.

We have been having a rain storm for the past two days. Diane went to camp yesterday with the girl scouts and dad is sick in bed. Right after I finish this letter I am going to write a letter to Mr. and Mrs. Carroll. I am being real good with the girls, there has hardly been any fights. Last night mom and I looked over all my literature and sorted it out. I am back to normal as far as school goes and I am starting to sleep until 6:30 in the morning.

Mon. Feb. 3, 1975

It is 7:30 and I am just waiting for breakfast. Mom is going to take this weekend off and we are going to look for cars. Mom doesn't know whether to get the Buick or the Oldsmobile. The Oldsmobile is bigger, it gets better gas mileage, and I like it. But mom says she has to see them both so that's why we are going this weekend. We will order it then and it will come right before my birthday, like it was my birthday present.

***

Jim Malan, 1975 May, 13 yrs old

Dear C _ _ _ _,

I couldn't find a card that said "congratulations" and "will miss you this summer," so I decided to write my own.

I sure was happy when we graduated, and yet, it was "kinda" sad about leaving the dump. That's the place that literally taught me all I know. Eight years of teaching, but I think it has done me some good. In fact, as I look back on the eight years some of it did seem fun (or at least it does now). We had a great bunch of teachers and I learned a lot from the other students. And you were the main one who taught me. I owe a lot to you. You helped me with things, you talked with me, you felt sad with me. That time I walked down the hall and outside with you, because Sister Joan got you upset really told me something about you. That you are fragile, yet strong, persistent yet resistant. Everyone, especially I think you're a great person and fun to be with. All I can really say is "Thank you very, very much for all you have done." I truly hope you have a great time on your cross-country trip. Be sure to write and always stay the way you are. You've got as good of future as any girl could ever dream of. I know you'll put your intelligence, know-how, and very powerful leadership into great use. You've got to.

Thanks again,

The President of your "fan club"

Jim

Jim Malan

154 Haven Hill Ct.

Danville, CA

P.S. Now you know why K _ _ _ _ _ thought my letters are so "corny."

1975 May

***

Tomb of The Unknowns post card (1975)

Dear Dad, Mom, Linda & Diane,

We saw the changing of the guard and sent through the Smithsonian Institution, Capital, and White House.

Love,

Jim and NaNa

***

St. Isidore's School

Jim Malan, Grade 8, Age 13

Week of Sept. 8, 75

English Journal

Yesterday, when I was walking my dog, I passed by a maple tree. It was windy. Some of the leaves were falling to the ground. I picked one up and examined it. It had little brown veins running through it. I wondered how it began. Suddenly it was snatched out of my hand by my dog. A pull on the leash told me she wanted to go and I followed.

Week of Sept. 15 1975

Yesterday was the worst school day that I have ever encountered. First off, I was nearly late for school. I couldn't find my homework because it was in my lunch. Then later in the morning I get in trouble for sitting back on my chair. The afternoon went by pretty well. But then I went home and forgot my home work. What a day.

Week of Sept. 22 1975

Today is just not my day. First, I forgot my P.E. clothes and my lunch. My P.E. box was broken and I have to pay $1.75 what a rip. This day should go in the book of world records.

Week of Sept. 29, 75

Today was great. We didn't have any home work. I scored the highest on my science test. I also got an "A" on my chapter structure. What a great day.

Week of Oct. 6, 75

Today it was warm so I went swimming in our pool. The water was crisp and cool. Overhead I could see the birds as they flew south for the winter. After swimming I walked my dog. What a day.

Week of Oct. 13, 75

Today I am excited, because after school we are going to see how our new house is coming along. It's supposed to be done next week, but I doubt that it will. They still have a lot of work to do.

Week of Oct 20, 75

Our house was supposed to be done today, but it wasn't. That figures! Every time I see the workers they are having a coffee break or playing cards. They better hurry up so we can move in.

Week of Oct. 27, 75

Today we went down to see our house after school. It's really coming along. They finally put up the shutters. The rugs and lights go in tomorrow. Boy I can't wait till we move in!

***

St. Isidore's School

Jim Malan, Sept. 12, '75, Age 13, Grade 8

Religion Quiz

1. Mohammed, Zoroaster, Confucius

2. "JC Superstar," says that Jesus was just a man, but today we know that he is risen and in heaven rather than dead and gone.

3a. Mosaics – picture Christ as stern and powerful.

3b. They all have pictures of people making fun of Jesus or as Jesus in a mean or stern fashion.

4. A nominal Christian is a person who says they are a Christian, but don't really know anything about God. They don't read the Bible or go to mass. They have sort of their "own" religion.

5. I would tell them that they can think what they want to think, and I'll think what I want to. They have their own beliefs and I have mine. He is my God, and he is what I believe in and what I want to believe in. I would tell them that they should look into my God and see what he's like. Then maybe they would have a different opinion about God.

***

St. Isidore's School

Jim Malan, Sept. 24 75, Age 13, Grade 8

Creative Writing

"Murray's Horse"

I didn't know what to do! I dropped the potatoes in the sink. One fell into the drain and blocked up the water, as the sink faucet was still pouring out lukewarm water.

As I went outside, I saw the paint rags on fire of which we had painted the stable. The fire had caught onto some dry weeds and spread to the stable.

I heard Buckwheat giving a snort that signaled that he knew something was wrong. The fire quickly crept up the stable wall and in a matter of seconds the cedar shake roof was alighted with hot blazing debris flying from it. This all happened so fast. I didn't know what to do.

I panicked. First, I ran and opened the door of the stable. There I saw Buckwheat eating some hay as though nothing had happened. I ran and grabbed a rope which I tied around his neck to lead him out of the fiery maze.

Suddenly a post fell giving way to part of the roof which fell on top of me. There I lay, still conscious with the sizzling fire just a few feet from me. Luckily, Buckwheat escaped the misfortune and was in a safe place. He knew that I was in danger. He came over to me. I grabbed the rope and said "Go." He pulled me out from under the beam and out of the stable. From there I crawled to safety. I heard some faint sirens and there was a crowd forming in our front yard. Some people down the road called the fire department. They came and put out the fire. I have to put up with a sprained ankle for a few days. I was sure glad that I talked my mom and dad into getting Buckwheat. He's the bravest horse that anyone could ever own.

The End

***

St. Isidore's School

Jim Malan Sept. 28, 1975, Age 13, Grade 8

Science—Current Events

The abnormal summer we had this past year.

As most of you know, this past year was a pretty weird summer. On the average, the Bay Area has 30 days above 100 degrees, 40 days from 80 to 99, and 20 days less than 80. Despite the belated snowfall in early March, the summer looked like it would be a hot one. It started off with a low one day of 73 degrees recorded at 1 o'clock in the morning. We had temperatures in the 80's and all the swimming pools opened up in early April. Towards the end of April, it started to cool off and get cloudy. The temperatures stayed around 60 for 3 weeks and then they started a slow climb up into the low 80's. In late May, the temperatures hit 93 and stayed that way for a week. Then they dropped. It rained on and off for 10 days with the temperature staying below 65. Also, the lowest temperature was recorded during this part of the summer. It dropped to 49 one night and most of the plants died. During the latter part of June, the temperatures stayed in the upper 70's. Then, the first week of July was a hot one. The temperatures started off in the low 90's and by the end of the week it was up to 109. The temperatures stayed this way for 2 weeks and then changed. They dropped into the 60's and it rained for 4 days. The weather stayed mild through August with the temperature not going beyond 85. Then came Indian Summer and the temperatures shot up into the 90's and stayed that way for 2 weeks. And on the first day of fall, the temperature was 101.

Comparing this year to last year: This year we had 30 days above 100 compared to 46 days last year. We had 40 days from 80 to 99 compared to 31 last year. And we had 20 days less than 80 compared to 19 last year. The record for the Bay Area still stands at 123.9 recorded on Concord on July 15 of last year. (1974)

***

St. Isidore's School

Jim Malan, Oct. 2, 1975, Age 13, Grade 8

The Power of Language

(Teacher's note: Terrific composition!)

Language is the most important thing that living things can develop. The art of language helps you in almost everything you need to do. Thought is the main thing to do with language. Without thought, you would not know what to say or do. Language developed many years ago when primitive man wanted to communicate with other beings. They developed a system which all the members knew. Each sound meant a specific thing. For example, "blopt" meant eat. Soon this system spread around the world. Then, later in the progression of language, someone else came up with another system of communication. This soon got around and soon, everyone was speaking this form of communication rather than the other one. But then someone said, "Why not use both of them? One part of the world could use one language and the other part could use the other language." The people thought that this was basically a good idea so they tried it, and it went over pretty good for a while. Then another man thought up a new means of communication and more men thought up different forms of communication and soon there were many languages. They were all spoken in different parts of the world. But each of these languages was very limited. There just weren't enough words for each symbol. This is where thought came in. People saw something. But they didn't know what to call it. So, they made up their own sound for it. All the people did this and naturally their sounds were different for various things. This caused a grave mix up and one day, a man called part of the world's population together and he set up a universal language system with some words from all the existing languages. The people soon learned this language and soon the whole world was communicating in their own tongue. But again, some man thought up different words and made up his own language and man men followed him and started the whole thing over again. But everything worked out and we now have many different languages but there is a word for everything. But language is much more than just words. There is a meaning behind every word so that other people can understand what one is saying. But people are not the only living things that have their own language. It is believed that many fish, porpoises, dolphins, and types of monkeys have their own special language. And with careful research and study, we can get them to understand our language and us to understand theirs. Language has power to do anything that the person who speaks it wills it to do. It can cheer up a person, or cut down a person. It can be spoken with meaning, or just off the top of your head. Language is the key to life that holds the world's communication in its letters. The ability to speak with someone or something.

Exactly <u>500</u> words………………………….yes………….

***

St. Isidore's School

Jim Malan, Oct. 15, 75, Age 13, Grade 8

Religion

My Creed

I believe in one God, who in his midst brought me to act out a daily life among my fellow brothers and sisters; who expected of me to do what I thought, in my own judgment, was the best thing to accomplish; who gave me the many talents which I and all my fellow beings possess and act out in our everyday lives, who gave me this chance to live on this earth and live a good life so that I could rejoin him in Heaven again some day. I believe in His Son, Jesus Christ, the Savior of my soul, who guides and helps me in all my actions, my triumphs and defeats; who came down upon this earth as a humble carpenter and died so that I could live; who gave me a chance to do what he did. I believe in one Holy Spirit, whom soon I shall receive for my second time very shortly. Who shall even give me more knowledge of how to live a good and spiritual life with my fellow man.

Most of all I believe in one most Holy Trinity, without which I would cease to exist; who show me the light of my life and who points out the good and bad things in it. Without them the world would not be a world, people would not be people, and I would not be me.

. . . . . Amen . . . . .

(Teachers note: I really feel like you mean what you say. Thanks!)

***

St. Isidore's School

Jim Malan, Oct. 28, 75, Age 13, Grade 8

Religion Test

1. So we could get to know him. All about how he was born, lived, performed great miracles. The editors wrote about Him so we could learn how to love and obey Him. Also, so we could see how people around the world react to him. He demands personal decisions, but within his guidance. He wants us to make our own decisions within ourselves so that we may be more open to his teachings.

4. The main idea that I observed from His teachings was that he was here on Earth to help us to know why WE are here, our purpose, and what we are expected of. He converted people to follow him as in the story of the stoning. He said, "All among you without sin may cast the first stone." Also when he called his apostles, who were devoted to their lives as fishermen, to follow him.

5. Self-knowledge is a key thing in a Christian's life because it lets him know what his inner feelings are and how to cope with them. We can know ourselves and how to and what to do with them so we can be closer to God by what we really are.

6. A saint is a person who during his life had so much love, devotion and trust in God, that he felt that God was alive and with them (which he is in a sense). It's not exactly a person with his head in the "Spiritual Clouds," but a person who communicates with other people about God. You could say that he is a nice guy type. He loves all people, whether sinners or followers and tries to show "God" in all his

actions. For instance, Saint Francis of Assisi loved God and all of his creations. Saint James the Greater loved his fellow man enough to die for him. St. John the Baptist was beheaded for the sake of mankind. Every saint had some special connection with God. We all are saints in our own special way.

***

3rd Quarter 1975

1. I just got back from vacation. Boy, did I have fun. We drove down to Mexico and bought some light fixtures and paintings. Then drove up to Disneyland and stayed there for a day. Then we took the long ride home. I slept most of the way. It was a fun vacation, but it was great to be home.

2. It's eight thirty sharp

It's time for school

I take off my tarp

And sit on my stool

The second bell rings,

We say our prayers.

My desk is a mess

But I don't care

The day passes by.

It's almost through

My shoe I tie

And . . . What I'll do.

3. Today we went on a field trip. It was fun. Mrs. "C" got lost on the way home because Mike gave her the wrong directions. We finally made it back. We were an hour late.

4. Next month I will be fourteen. I can't wait. Then I'll be in high school. Then college. Then I'll get married. Then I'll get a job. Then I'll . . .

5. Tonight, I got a ton of home work. I had track and an appointment after school. Now here I am at 7:30 writing this 30zxs journal. What a bore. Oh well, that's life.

6. Next month starts swim season. Only a few more weeks, I can't believe it. This year I'll be on the Sycamore Swim Team since I moved. They are pretty good. My sister and I can't wait.

7. School is almost over I can tell, spring is already upon us. The trees are blossoming. People are wearing short sleeve shirts and shorts. Summer sports are appearing. The signs tell.

8. Homework!!! This word persists to tear me apart. It's driving me mad! Homework!!! Why do we have it? Why does it exist? It surges on until you can't take it anymore. You give in and miss an assignment.

9. I am done with my journal.

The quarter is done.

Summer's almost here.

It signals some fun.

A diary of thoughts.

I leave to you

Grade them truthfully,

And pardon my boo boo's.

***

New Quarter

A few days ago I went to San Francisco International Airport. As we drove by it, I could see the monstrous snake like tubes. When we went into the terminal, I saw many people running aimlessly, rushing, talking, all going in different directions. Overhead, I heard roaring sounds and the whole airport shook, as a jet roared over the airport. I got to shake hands with a captain. It's amazing how a few humans can pilot such a huge monster.

2. Today is Saturday. This has to be the most boring day I've ever spent. I sat out in the garage for eight hours straight. I was helping my dad build a loft. It looked good when it was done, but it was hard work.

3. Today we had our weekly student council meeting. We got a lot done. I said the prayers, C _ _ _ called the meeting to order. Katie read the minutes, and we were under way. We decided on some programs and finally completed our agenda. P _ _ _ said the final prayer, and we all went into the library.

4. It's school time. I just got my name on the board for being out of my seat, but I have an excuse!! I was raising the flags. Well there's fifty words I don't have to do.

5. Today my dog almost got run over. I was so scared as she ran out into the street. This man came speeding along. He slowed down but was still rolling toward Bambi. But Bambi's a smart dog. Just when the car was reaching her, she turned her head and just missed getting run over. Relief!!

6. Wow, it's warm today! People are out playing around. It's like summer. I feel like swimming. Too bad I can't. Oh well, I can't wait till summer. Meanwhile I hope it snows.

7. Poem

I'm done with my journal

Hooray for me

I hear a whistle

The cup of tea

I close up my book

I really am done

It's time for me,

To have some fun

I thought I was done

My face was happy

But, I'm not done

I still have some more.

I'm done!!

***

The Story of the Nativity

By James Malan

Narrator: This is the story of the first Christmas. The actors are as follows:

The Presentation Angels are:

Gabriel

Joseph

Mary

Three Kings

Four Shepherds

Three Innkeepers

Narrator

Elizabeth

Presentation Angels: This is a play about the birth of our Lord. We hope you will enjoy it.

Narrator: It was in Bethlehem a long time ago. Joseph was at work and Mary was picking flowers.

Angel: I am Gabriel sent from the Lord, fear not for thus the Lord has said he wishes you to be the Mother of his son Jesus Christ.

Mary: Why I shall be happy to be the Mother if that is what thy father wants.

Angel: And behold thy cousin Elizabeth will have a son of the same age.

Mary: Oh! I must go see her.

Narrator: And the Angel departed from her, and Mary ran to tell Joseph.

Mary: An Angel has told me we shall be the parents of the Lord. I also must go see my cousin Elizabeth.

Joseph: So, she is to have a baby too?

Mary: Yes.

Narrator: Mary leaves for her cousin's house.

Mary: (Knocks on Elizabeth's door)

Elizabeth: Mary! Why did you come?

Mary: An Angel told me you were to have a baby.

Elizabeth: That was very kind of you to come.

Mary: I am to be the Mother of the Lord, the Angel has said so.

Elizabeth: Oh! I am so happy for you.

Mary: Thank you. What are you going to name him?

Mary: I'm back.

Joseph: How was Elizabeth?

Mary: She was happy about her baby and mine too.

Narrator: Mary and Joseph go to sleep. Then it becomes morning.

Mary: We better look for a place where the baby can be born. There is not enough room in our house.

Joseph: You are right we will start looking now.

Narrator: They both start packing for them and the baby and leave by afternoon.

Mary: I think I see an inn down the road, let's check there.

Joseph: (Knocks) Do you have any room in your inn? My wife is going to give birth to God, our father's son, Jesus Christ.

1st Innkeeper: No, we are all filled up. But there is another inn about another 10 miles along the road.

Joseph: That will take us almost all night. Is there one closer?

1st Innkeeper: I'm sorry, but that's the closest one.

Joseph: Well, thank you anyway.

Narrator: Joseph and Mary continue to walk for hours until they come to an inn.

Joseph: (Knocking) Do you have a room for us just for the night?

2nd Innkeeper: I'm sorry, we are all filled up. But there is an inn about six miles down the road. They might have room.

Joseph: Thank you very much.

Narrator: By now, Joseph and Mary are very tired for they have been walking all day. But still they keep traveling on.

Joseph: There it is. You stay here while I go check.

Mary: Alright.

Joseph: (Knocking) Do you happen to have a room for the night?

3rd Innkeeper: I am so sorry. We are all filled up. Every room. But there is a manger in a little shack with animals in it. I could let you have that.

Joseph: Oh thank you.

3rd Innkeeper: It is right down the road.

Narrator: Joseph returns to Mary.

Joseph: There were all filled up, but he said we could use the manger. It is right down the road.

Narrator: Joseph and Mary arrive at the manger and give birth to the Lord.

"SILENT NIGHT"

Now we go to a hillside on which there are four shepherds and their sheep. And suddenly they hear music and three angels appear.

Angels: Behold, we bring you tidings of great joy. For the Lord our God shall be born in Bethlehem this night. You go to the manger. The star will guide you.

"O COME ALL YE FAITHFUL"

Narrator: The shepherds start walking and they bring some sheep. Soon they reach the manger.

1st Shepherd: Is this the infant?

Joseph: Yes it is.

4th Shepherd: He's – He's beautiful.

2nd Shepherd: We bring you these lambs.

Mary: Thank you.

3rd Shepherd: We should all kneel down and thank the Lord for this night.

Narrator: Now on another hillside we find three kings. They are amazed by the shining star.

1st King: Look at that beautiful star!

2nd King: It gives one a feeling he can't express.

3rd King: Let us follow it and see where it shall lead us.

Narrator: The kings follow the star and soon come to the manger also.

"WE THREE KINGS"

2nd King: Why, it leads us to a manger with a tiny infant.

3rd King: We shall go to the camel and get gifts for the wonderful child.

Narrator: The kings go and come back with presents of gold, silver and myrrh. Then they kneel down in prayer.

Joseph: Thank you very much.

Narrator: And they all continued in prayer. So ends the story of the Nativity of our Lord. We hope you have enjoyed it.

"WE WISH YOU A MERRY CHRISTMAS"

1975

***

Binder #2

1976 8th Grade

Promise Yourself

PROMISE yourself to be so strong that nothing can disturb your peace of mind. To talk health, happiness and prosperity to every person you meet. To make all your friends feel that there is something in them. To look at the sunny side of everything and make your optimism come true. To think only of the best. To work only for the best and expect only the best. To be just as enthusiastic about the success of others as you are about your own. To forget the mistakes of the past and press on to the greater achievements of the future. To wear a cheerful countenance at all times and give every living creature you meet a smile. To give so much time to the improvement of yourself that you have no time to criticize others. To be too large for worry, too noble for anger, too strong for fear and too happy to permit the presence of trouble.

Found in Jim's papers

***

Jim Malan, Grade 8, 1976

"Creative Writing"

Homework

The teacher tried everything under the sun. That he hoped would make me get my homework done. But try as he may, he never succeeded, because of the books, that I never read.

He'd try apples and candy and teddy bears too. Sports cars and tractors, a brand new banjo, jackets and sweaters and pure woolen socks, ice cream and cookies and bagels with lox.

Flowers and post cards and monkeys and cats. Horses and hamsters, yes even grey rats. And even today, that stupid old teacher wants to give up and become an old preacher. If only he knew that back in that day, all that I wanted was one stupid "A."

***

Pleasures as an Animal

X = the dog, free frisky—romping in a wide open field

On a clear day

No cares, worries responsibilities, etc. Just free

No one exists, but the dog and the rolling hills

Jim Malan, 1976 Grade 8

***

Treasures on Diablo

X = me, sitting on a high rock, looking out over the Diablo Valley watching life ramble on below me.

Gives me a sense of power and intelligence knowing with one sweep of my eyes, I can see so many people, hours of work, happiness and life

Jim Malan, 1976 Grade 8

***

Creative Writing

Jim Malan 1976

Inside a steamy pool at 5:30 AM, you will find the swimmer. The dedicated youngster is seen swimming, back and forth, hundreds upon hundreds of grueling laps. Once in a great while, you will see him stop to unfog his goggles, but only for an instant. After two hours in the water, he will get out, dry his bleached hair and sun burnt skin, and ready himself for school. The swimmer leads two very active, but rewarding lives.

During school, the swimmer has to "keep up" with the rest of the class. Being a swimmer is no excuse for slacking off in studies. At lunch the swimmer is usually seen in the library getting a start on his homework for that night. Immediately following school, he goes directly to the pool where he will swim for two more hours. After this, he goes home, eats a well balanced protein enriched dinner and does his homework.

After homework he does various exercises and muscle strengtheners for about an hour. Bedtime is as early as possible, no later than 9:30 PM.

As a result of this awesome schedule, the swimmer has very little time for his social life. He must practice at least six days a week. Very few swimmers have jobs. There just isn't time.

Probably the greatest disappointment that the swimmer has is the amount of time he has to his family. This amount is extremely small. But if it wasn't for his gracious parents who so readily drive him anywhere and constantly encourage him, the swimmer wouldn't exist.

The swimmer is definitely a unique person. Unique in the way that he is truly dedicated to the sport. Swimming becomes the major part of his life. To be successful, in swimming the swimmer must dedicate himself to hard work, disappointments, long hours, and personal commitment.

***

Jim Malan, 1974, 14 yrs. old

<u>The Swimmer</u>

Training, working, always in the water, bleached hair, tired, competing, striving and setting goals. Physically fit, constantly thinking about swimming, competitive, restless, love of the water and early practices. Long practices, early to bed, very early to rise. Has to keep up with school. Little welcomed free time, being called weird, struggling, kind parents, always on the go. Loving to be tired. Used to a heavy schedule. Taking vitamins to guard against colds. Never seeing family. Eating well, but irregular. Less social activities.

***

Creative Writing

I REMEMBER

I remember living in a massive house

    And falling down the stairs

I remember walking to kindergarten

    And tripping

I remember riding my bike with training wheels

    And crying when I fell

I remember getting M&Ms from my grandmother

    And choking on them

I remember teasing my cat

    And screaming when she bit me

I remember trying to act older and stay up late

    And crying when my mom put me down

I remember carrying my sister around the house

    And getting yelled at when I dropped her

I remember dreaming about my future

    And being disappointed because it came too fast

Jim Malan, Grade 8, 1976

***

Mr. Calhoun

Science

Cardiac Murmurs: The Causes and Effects

Jim Malan, Mar. 22, 1976 8th grade, St. Isidore's School, 14 yrs. old

Outline

I. What is a Cardiac Murmur?

  A. Characteristics

  B. Symptoms

    1. Children

    2. Adults

  C. Functions

    1. Positive

    2. Negative

  D. Causes

II. When and How They Appear.

  A. Diseases

    1. Rheumatic Fever

      a) Systolic Rheumatic Fever

      b) Diastolic Rheumatic Fever

    2. Pneumonia

    3. Valvular Disease

  B. At Birth

  C. Early Childhood

  D. Adulthood

  E. After Strenuous Exercise

III. Affects on the Body.

  A. Abnormal Circulation

  B. Abnormal Heartbeat

  C. Valves

  D. Restrictions

  E. Fatality

IV. All Specific Murmurs.

  A. Characteristics

  B. Symptoms

  C. Diagnosis

V. Care of Murmurs in General.

  A. Amount of Exercise

    1. Marsh Murmurs

    2. Harmless Murmurs

  B. Restrictions

  C. After Heart Attack

  D. After Strenuous Exercise

VI. Case History

VII. Conclusion

Cardiac murmurs: An abnormal heart sound found in over 30% of mankind. A soft blowing sound caused by an incompetent valve vibrating from the push of blood passing by it. A murmur may be harmless, yet serious, depending on the kind of murmur and the conditions in which it exists. Through various books and pamphlets and one case study, I will present, in full, information concerning cardiac murmurs; the functions, types, causes, and effects on the body as a whole, and in sections. Whether harmless, or serious, a murmur can alter the life of a single human being. They are just another "half-known" problem of our complex body, which has no cure as of yet.

The heart beat consists of seven to ten sounds, depending on the rate of the beat. These sounds are graphed by a machine called an electrocardiogram (EKG). This machine creates a diagram similar to the one pictured here. . . This picture shows how fast the heart is beating and if any abnormalities exist.

A murmur is usually caused by an incompetent valve, but it can be caused by blockage in an artery or blood turbulence in the great vessels. It appears before or after one of the heart sounds and usually delays the sound in the process.

Children are the ones who usually acquire cardiac murmurs, but in some cases, murmurs may appear in adults also. A murmur has symptoms just as a common cold does. Symptoms in a child are probably different from symptoms in an adult. In a child (up to late adolescence) shortage of breath, abnormal heart beat, and occasional hyperactivity are among the major symptoms.

In an adult, the major symptoms of a cardiac murmur are a pain in the chest near the sternum (various murmurs), tiredness, and an abnormal heard beat. The adult with a murmur usually has a much greater chance to acquire some other form of heart disease.

Despite the murmur being a disease, it also has various functions. The positive functions are: when for some reason the heart beat is unusually low, a murmur may appear to help speed up the heart beat so blood may circulate at a quicker rate. Also, if there is a piece of tissue or a foreign object caught in your blood stream, the murmur gives the blood an "extra boost" which may dislodge the object. The negative portion of a murmur's functions vastly outweighs that of the positive. Among the functions on the list are: abnormal breathing, abnormal heart beat, slower or faster than normal circulation of blood, tiredness, and light headedness. Not every murmur possesses these qualities but most of them have some sort of effect on the way the body "ticks." Also, a murmur throws the whole body off balance. The blood is circulated at an abnormal rate, not depositing enough oxygen in the blood, causing delay of oxygen to the organs and delaying the process all over again. (This can be compared to the hypothalamus not secreting enough thyroid stimulating hormone and finally ending up with an abnormal effect on thyroid.)

Murmurs may appear during and/or after some form of disease. Rheumatic fever is the most known disease to produce heart problems, sometimes cardiac murmurs. There are two types of rheumatic fever that contend with heart murmurs: systolic rheumatic fever and diastolic rheumatic fever. Systolic rheumatic fever occurs when the chambers of the heart are in the act of pumping the blood out the pulmonary artery or aorta. The blood "snags" on a piece of tissue on the sides of one of these vessels which creates a "lubb" sound which is referred to as a murmur.

Systolic Rheumatic Fever

Diastolic Rheumatic Fever

Diastolic rheumatic fever that presents a murmur occurs when the blood fills the left and right atriums. The blood snags on a piece of tissue inside the pulmonary vein or vena-cava. This blood is forced into the protrusion and creates the murmur.

Pneumonia is also another disease that contributes to cardiac murmurs. This infection clogs the great vessels around the heart with a mucous-like material. Blood has to pass through at a slower rate because of this. When the heart pumps, the chambers are not fully filled with blood and as a result, the murmur is heard as a "hollow" sound.

Probably the disease that most causes cardiac murmurs is valvular disease. This is when either the tricuspid, pulmonary, mitral or aortic valves are malfunctioning in some manner. They either delay the blood to be pumped or not fully close, allowing blood to "slide" through that is not supposed to. This can cause a major problem, for the blood could flow in the opposite direction thus demolishing the entire circulation system.

Cardiac murmurs, severe or not, may have numerous effects on the body. The most obvious one is abnormal heart beat. The murmur delays, slows down, or speeds up the beat of the heart. This leads into another effect murmurs have on the body: abnormal circulation. Since the heart beat is changed, the circulation is abnormal, either sending blood too rapidly or two slowly. This either puts too much blood to different organs or not enough. Also, murmurs that aren't caused by the valves affect the valves in a certain way. If the beat is delayed, the valves have to "let through" more blood than usual. This puts a strain on the valves and soon could develop into some heart problem. Along with some murmurs come lifelong restrictions. Little exercise, special diet, regular checkups and early bedtimes are a few of these. After the murmur disappears (if it does) these restrictions can slowly be lifted.

A very small percentage of cardiac murmurs cause death. Death occurs when the heart is totally malfunctioning and surgery is no cure or assistance. This usually occurs in children between the ages of 6 months and 5 years.

There are many kinds of specific murmurs. Now that you have a pretty good outline on murmurs, here are a few of the hundreds of specific murmurs known to us today . . .

1. ANEUHYSMAL: A wheezing systolic sound heard with and after the first heart sound.

2. REGURGITATNT: Blowing, hissing sound. Heard after the second heart sound.

3. AORTIC OBSTRUCTIVE: A harsh systolic sound, heard after the third heart sound.

4. APEX: A very short murmur only found in rare cases. It is found over the apex of the heart.

5. ARTERIAL: A soft, flowing sound that is synchronized with the pulse.

6. BRONCHIAL: A murmur heard over the bronchi. It is more prominent in inhalation.

7. CARDIAC PULMONARY: This murmur is caused by the heart rubbing against the lungs.

8. DIASTOLIC: This murmur is caused when the heart decreases in size.

9. DIRECT: This murmur is caused when the blood en route to the heard is blocked and it has to travel around the obstruction.

10. ENDOCARDIAL: This murmur occurs when the force or "pump" of the heart isn't strong enough to get all the blood out of the heart or into the next chamber.

11. EXOCARDIAL: A murmur produced outside the cavities of the heart. Usually found in the blood vessel of the aorta.

12. FRICTION: This murmur is caused when inflamed mucous surfaces inside the heart are rubbing.

13. FUNCTIONAL: This murmur is the most common found in children. It is a harmless murmur that appears during a common cold and disappears after is has ended. It may also be present at birth but is soon grown out of. Cause: when the heart is a little larger in relation to the valves or the valves are a little smaller in relation to the heart. Blood passes through tiny cracks between the valves and the wall of the heart. This creates the "slushy" sound called the murmur.

14. HEMIC: A murmur that results from an anemic blood condition. The blood becomes thinner and "slides" through the valves rather than being pumped.

15. INDIRECT: A murmur heard when the blood flow is in abnormal directions, backwards through the valves, etc.

16. INORGANIC: When the cause of the murmur isn't due to structural changes.

17. MACHINERY: This is a continuous, rough murmur usually found in rheumatic disease patients.

18. MITRAL: Blood rushing through the mitral or bicuspid valves at an abnormal rate.

19. ORGANIC: A murmur caused by structural changes.

20. PERICARDIAL: A murmur produced within the pericardium (the thin membrane that encloses the heart).

21. PSYOLOGIC: A form of functional murmur. (see #13)

22. PRESYSTOLIC: A murmur producing a sound right before the heard contracts.

23. PULMONARY: A murmur produced from abnormalities at the entrance to the pulmonary artery.

24. REGURGITANT: The backward flow of blood through the heart. Always fatal.

25. SYSTOLIC: A murmur heard during the contraction of the heart. Caused by some form of obstruction.

26. TO AND FRO: This murmur is heard during both systole and diastole (contraction and expansion of heart).

27. TRICUSPID: A murmur occurring within the tricuspid blood vessels. Narrowing, obstruction, etc.

28. VESICULAR: A murmur heard during and caused by normal breathing.

Exercise is a main factor while in possession of a murmur. Depending on the murmur, exercise can either resume as normal, have mild restrictions, or have strict restrictions. With most murmurs, normal activities may resume. Some murmurs have mild restrictions which don't affect the normal activities of a person too much. Murmurs found in adults almost always have strict restrictions that must be followed exactly because the heard is very weak. Murmurs don't have to be constantly watched over but they shouldn't be totally ignored. A person with a cardiac murmur, in most cases, can be as active as a person without a murmur.

If a murmur occurs after a heart attack, special precautions should be taken. Walking should become part of the daily routine. Bi-weekly checkups are a must. A murmur after a heart attack is very risky because it greatly increases the chances of acquiring another heart attack.

A murmur may appear to become worse after continuous strenuous exercise. To a certain point, this may prove true. But usually, the murmur is just noticed by the person and seems louder to them.

CASE HISTORY

I have had a functional murmur since birth. I have had no restrictions whatsoever, but at times, it has seemed to have gotten bad. One night last summer, I was out swimming in our pool. I was real tired when I came in, so I got changed and went right to bed. A few minutes later, I had a funny feeling in my chest. It came again and again. I knew something was wrong with my heart. I felt as though it were "skipping" beats. After each time I felt this uncomfortable sensation, I was short of breath so I had to take a quick deep breath. My pulse was very abnormal. The next day I went to a cardiologist at Children's Hospital in Oakland. There, I had numerous x-rays and an EKG. The doctor said that the previous event the night before wasn't exactly normal but it wasn't severely abnormal. He said that it can happen after prolonged exercise and not to be too alarmed.

Murmurs have only been known to exist for 75 years. Doctors have learned little about murmurs since then. Students studying in the field of cardiology are constantly finding out new bits and pieces of information about these "sounds." Someday there may be a cure. Someday there may be a definite treatment. No one can tell. Murmurs could be very useful in some cases but knowledge is lacking on how to use them. People with very slow heart beat could use murmurs to speed their heart beat up to normal. The problem is: how to create an artificial cardiac murmur???? These problems will soon be solved. Cardiac murmurs are just a fragment of the unsolved problems about the heart that confront doctors, as well as patients. Murmurs are livable diseases that can pose unnecessary problems that could be corrected if further knowledge was known about the heart. But we don't have the needed knowledge!!! Research still continues: and soon, one day, in a quiet science anatomy lab, a scientist will be finishing an experiment on a cadaver and say something like "Eureka, I have found it!!" And from then on, cardiac murmurs will be a problem and an experience of the past.

***

Jim Malan, May 20, 1976, Age 14, Grade 8

St. Isidore's School

English

1. Today we went to buy my mom's birthday present. We got her a gift certificate from McCulloch's. She always complains that she doesn't have enough clothes. This will give her a great opportunity to relieve us from her complaining.

2. Today is her birthday (May 21). We went to the bakery to get the cake. Boy, does it look good! Chocolate with nuts on it. She was so surprised with the gift certificate we gave her, she will buy some clothes so she can have something to wear to my graduation.

3. My sisters are brats! They always get me in trouble. It's sickening. I try to help them out, and they don't even appreciate it. Why did I have to get stuck with these two . . . people. If I had my way for one day, I'd sure show them whose boss.

4. Only seven more days, then I'm home free. I have so much homework during these last weeks. I have swim team from four to six. I come home, water the garden, feed the dog, and eat dinner. By this time it is eight o'clock. Then I slave over my desk for a few hours. By the time I'm done, I'm too tired to watch TV.

5.
This world will self destruct without faith." This poster bugs me. It shows a picture of the earth "cracking up." Yuck! I guess there is some truth to it. If we don't have faith in one another, we will "fall apart."

6. This year is over.

Phew, what a year.

Summer is coming.

No more pain in the rear.

June is upon us.

July's almost here.

But soon comes September.

And begins the school year.

***

58

Jim Malan, Freshman, Sept. 20 '76

<u>English</u>

The three counselors are Mr. "H," Brother "T," and Mr. "A." Mr. "A" briefed us on the various guidance aspects. They were career guidance, college, personal and academia. He told us that he counsels the students whose last name begins with "A" through "G." He told us that all of the teachers are available for counseling at any time.

Next, Br. "T" . . . talked to us about the retreat program and his job as a counselor. He counsels people whose last name begins with "H" through "O." He explained the retreats and told us that they are to clear our minds, and help us relate to others.

Bro "J" . . . talked to us about campus ministry. How other children in this area like to feel important and cared for, that the toy drive helps, accomplish this.

Mr. "H" . . . said he is open to anyone as a teacher or counselor and will help anyone at any time.

***

Jim Malan, Dec. 12, '76

<u>Religion</u>

1. What is the miracle that happens?

The miracle comes when Helen feels the water from the pump. Her face changes. The muscles around her lips start to work. She stands puzzled. Then, a babyish sound is heard. "Wah-wah." The remembrance of her childhood returns. "Wah-wah." She knows. She spells it to Annie. She then pats the ground. She knows that it has a name, that it is something. Annie spells it to her. Helen spells back. Yes, the miracle happens. Helen understands what things are.

2. What is meant by "miracle" in this play?

The word "miracle" in this play means—something that people thought could not be done, is done. That "something" was making Helen understand. No one thought that Helen could ever understand what things were. No one believed that Helen would ever be able to communicate. But despite their disbelief, Helen did understand and could communicate. The impossible became possible, and so was thought to be a miracle.

3. How was Annie's background helpful in getting through to Helen?

Annie had once been blind herself. She knew how it felt. She knew how she learned to overcome the handicap. She had lived at a school where they taught blind children so she was familiar with the various techniques of instruction. She knew the terror of the asylum and didn't want Helen to have to face that. She had been blind and lived with the blind. All these experiences were combined to help Helen.

4. Was it really important that Annie could identify with Helen?

Yes. If Annie had not been blind, and suffered in her learning, she would not have known what and why Helen was feeling and acting the way she was. Annie knew that it took persistence, patience, and little pity to make Helen respect her. When this respect was accomplishs, the way was clear for making Helen understand.

5. What is wrong in the relationship between James and Capt. Keller?

Their relationship is not that of a father and son. It is more like the relationship between a hated boss and stubborn employee. I think that the Captain has expected a lot more out of James since Helen can't do much. James sees this burden and rebels. And when James tries to be good, he just gets put down all the more. If the Captain took a close look at the situation, he would see that he should start treating James as his son; not as one of his troops.

6. What is the outcome of that relationship?

The outcome is a true father-son relationship. When Helen "acted up" again at the dinner table after the two weeks with Annie, James showed the Captain that he was wrong. James had listened to the Captain all his life and agreed with him whether he was right or wrong. This time, the Captain was wrong and James told him this. The astonished, speechless Captain could not do anything but glare at him. After the miracle, when dinner resumed, the Captain nodded to James in approval. He realized now that this is his son. He realized that if it wasn't for this son of his, that Helen might still be the uncontrollable animal that she has been for the past years.

7. What is the significance of the keys?

The keys are Helen's way of saying that Annie is a great person and that she cares about her very much. The keys open the door that Annie was trying to open for so long: The door to Helen's respect. And now,

Helen presents the keys to Annie and in doing this, presenting her respect to her also. The door is now open, respect and love is now contacted, the teacher and the student, now communicating.

8. What was Annie's belief concerning discipline?

Annie knew that a child had to be disciplined before he/she could show respect. And show respect before he/she could learn. Without discipline, the respect and understanding are impossible. This is why she insisted on obedience.

9. In terms of Religious Experience, how is what happed with Helen similar to the process of religious faith?

Annie believed that Helen could understand; she knew Helen must understand. Her persistence and little pity went into this belief. The fights, quarrels, hurting moments, all contributed to this belief. The hours of talking, spelling, waiting, all supported this belief, until the belief turned into a reality, and a dumb wild animal turned into a child with human understanding.

Religious faith is somewhat along this line. We believe in God. We spend many hours going to church to praise him. In other countries there have been quarrels and hurting moments from people with religious faith. We believe that this faith will turn into reality we can witness—when Christ comes again.

***

Thur. Dec. 18, '76

Dear you Guys,

Yesterday we went to New York. PopPop dropped us off t the United Nations Building. After we got out, NaNa realized that she had PopPop's money in her hand and he didn't have a cent. We didn't know what to do. We got in a cab and started chasing him. Soon out of sight he was. The taxi man was nice and kept telling us that everything would be alright. We turned a corner and there was PopPop a few cars in front of us. We chased him for 5 minutes, dodging traffic lights. There was much traffic. He finally had a red light. NaNa and I jumped out, ran through the traffic and caught him just in time. He was shocked. We ran back to the cab and went back to the U.N. We spent hours there. We went into the Assembly room and saw the last General Assembly of the year. We took a tour through the whole U.N. I got a solid bronze coin and some literature. We ate lunch in the cafeteria. Then we got a cab to the Empire State Building. The weather was good and we could see up to 80 miles. Then we walked from 34th Street all the way up 5th Avenue, to 50th Street. We stopped at B. Altman's Lord and Taylor Sachs 5th Ave. We went to Rockefeller Center to see the ice-skaters. Then we went to St. Patrick's Cathedral and then to the top of the sixes where we met PopPop for dinner. The cheapest thing on the menu was $7.50. I got broiled steak with a salad, grapefruit, tomato juice, ice cream or soufflé and Shirley Temple. We had a window seat looking down at 5th Ave. Earlier this week we went to the Smithville Inn where we saw Terry. Mr. Kraus called and I am going there tomorrow. The organ just came. It is snowing lightly. Send out some Phisohex!!! Keep this letter. Can't wait to see you.

Love

Jim,

NaNa,

PopPop

Merry Christmas

***

1962-1976

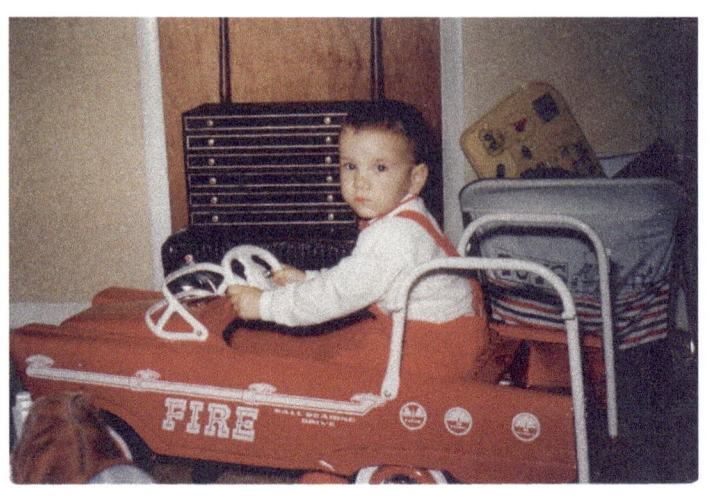

James Malan

Dear Mom and Dad,
A very happy and holy joyous Christmas to you. I love you and will pray to the Lord Jesus for you.
Love James

'68

Binder #3

1977

LIFE IS NEVER BORING!

Life . . . boring—no way life could ever be boring. If for a moment you think that life is boring do not speak that you feel this way because a friend might be inclined to help you out of this boredom in a very unusual manner. Watch out!!! The sky is falling but the sun still stands; it is strong.

The sun rose in the east and so he too chose to rise there. It is June, 1977; let's go back He was a small boy, led a simple life, was born April 27th, what a day the world would see!!! Had a nice family, was lucky, but were they in turn so lucky? He lived quiet, while young, gathered thoughts as ammunition—what a mind was growing—what a mind!!! Lived in New Jersey, used to go to a pizza parlor there. He liked this place—then he was five. Life went on, moved to the west. Directions changed. He grew, school was good, got excellent grades, parents were proud. Discovered music. What a time it was! Played the organ for years and years. Was very good, and sang too. He sang at school and at home, for himself and for others. Life was a song and he sang his life. Well, soon he dropped his early years and was an upper classman. Was Commissioner of Religious Affairs. Still he sang: the theme from Mahogany, As the Saints Go Marching In! And sometimes it got him 5 points off or 10 or maybe a piece of flying chalk. But he added to craziness and with these added things it grew. And soon he graduated. He went to high school still singing and crazy. He had fun and was a success. I thought for a while he had forgotten; weird but he hadn't. The year went fast—Two Gentlemen was great. He was singing pleased and crazy. And still he is; as one tin soldier rides away.

Confuse yourself, laugh and let's be free or else life will be boring, and believe me, life is never boring.

***

Jim Malan 15 yrs. old, 1977

> In that place
>
> The wind prevailed
>
> Sound was always
>
> Wind heaved through the pines past the cliffs
>
> The pines tremble mourning the memory
>
> Of the wind
>
> ***

Jim Malan, 1977

IV

The people that opposed the New Deal policies were the courts. Both the people and the legislature were pleased with the New Deal because it had started the economy rolling. However, the courts put a stop to the bill passing. They accused Roosevelt of Communism because they thought he was controlling too much and too many of the businesses. They tried to scare him by refusing to pass his bills. This soon stopped when Roosevelt requested the age limit on the Supreme Court. I'm seeing this Executive vs. Legislative battle. Some of the people rose to tell Roosevelt that he was acting in a Communistic manner. The courts blamed Roosevelt for these uprisings. They accused him of being too liberal for the economy's good.

***

Jim Malan, 1977

Objective

The traffic policeman has a job which is both tiring and dangerous. He stands in the middle of a very busy intersection eight hours a day. His hands are constantly moving, conveying signals to waiting motorists. His whistle is constantly adding to the already too noisy environment, as he blows it incessantly. He directs traffic in the rain and snow as well as the scorching heat. He risks his life each minute that he stands amidst the endless surge of traffic. Occasionally exciting even fraught with danger the night police patrol lonely and routine filled with endless hours of checking, watching, patrolling and writing reports. Endless reports.

15 yrs. old

***

Jim Malan, 1977, 15 yrs old

Writing

"Persuasive"

I think that the many faithful (traffic policemen) of their city deserve the reasonable raise that they have requested. They stand in the center of the major intersections of the city, tirelessly and patiently directing traffic. They work in all kinds of weather, eight hours a day. They are constantly on their feet with nothing more than a lunch break for a rest. Their job is both thankless and monotonous not to mention the danger aspect that is involved. Contrary to what the majority of the motorists think, these men feel that they are making a substantial contribution to society.

I feel this way also. This is why I think that their request for a raise should be reconsidered.

***

Jim Malan, Feb 14, 1977, Freshman

Social Studies

"Sex Discrimination in America Today"

From the beginning there has always been sex discrimination. Maybe not as we know it today, but sex discrimination still exists. Males were always expected to do certain jobs and females were always expected to do certain jobs. Both males and females were expected to act a certain way. Males and females still have certain "ways" of living and acting today, but not like they have in the past.

Within the past ten years, women have started to take a stand and claim their rights. They have fought, argued and did just about anything to get attention; to get their message across to the men that "all people are created equal." Women have made this point. They fought to vote, they fought for a place in the government, they have fought to join cub scouts, boy scouts, participate in Little League, soccer and hockey. They have made their mark in professional and amateur sports. They have become priests, military officers, leaders and technicians. Women have shown that they can play the same role in society as a man does. Probably the greatest feat accomplished by women is their participation in the military. Since the draft has stopped (1973) the numbers of women enlisting in the military has doubled. They are winning equal status and recognition with male servicemen, admirals, lieutenants and even generals. Women are advancing the military ranks. Because of their excellence in the military, women are now encouraged to join. More academies are welcoming women with open arms. They are continually moving "up" in the military and they are very pleased, but according to them "they have a long way to go."

Yes, women are getting the recognition they want, but in some cases, it is going too far. They are beginning to think men are inferior. They are gaining the same view men once had of them. They are causing what is known as "reverse discrimination." Civil rights laws are being perverted to discriminate against males instead of just to prevent or correct bias against women. Many employers are hiring women even if some men are better qualified, just to say they are an "equal opportunity employer." It has been easier to hire women than to justify hiring more men. People see this as "reverse discrimination" taking place. Many cases of reverse discrimination are being brought to the courts. People are saying it is a violation of the Constitution's "equal protection clause." With all these "false hirings" taking place, employers are being forced to end their stereotypes and hire on capabilities, i.e. not for social recognition.

Women are moving "up" in society, but not all men have conceded to their wishes and not all women think that they should be "too equal." Most women are more comfortable being the minority than men are. Most men regard themselves as leaders (when women are present) and work better in male groups. Being a leader is difficult for most women and therefore they tend to be followers. Women also tend to work better in all female groups.

Even known women seem to look strong and seem completely different than their stereotype. They use their "feminine tactics" to get their way. They will always be the helpless ones while men will always take a stand. In fact, most men and women do behave in the stereotyped ways. They have been behaving a certain way all their life; it's too hard to change now. In my opinion, there will always be some form of sex discrimination as long as there are two sexes. One will always try to accomplish more than the other, but basically, they will live in the "stereotyped laws" set down ever since the beginning.

References

1. Psychology Today Oct 1976, "Minority more comfortable for women than men"

2. Psychology Today Oct 1976, "How women get their way"

3. U.S. New & World Report 3/29/'76, "Reverse Discrimination: Has it gone too far?"

4. U.S. News & World Report 6/28/'76, "Sex barrier: It's falling fast in the military"

***

Jim Malan, April 21, 1977

English (short story)

"50 Freestyle"

He dove, his body streamlined to the horizon. Gracefully he slipped into the cool inviting water. After a smooth long glide he started stroking, his huge muscular arms churning through the water, splashing droplets through the air. His feet were kicking steadily, creating a wake behind him, as a motorboat does. Within seconds he turned. His long, slender feet came over the top of him while his body somersaulted underneath the water. His feet touched the side and propelled the streamlined body in the opposite direction in which he had come. His body became a human machine once more, as he pulled himself toward the wall ahead of him. He touched his legs, touched the bottom and he slowly stood up, brushing his hair out of his face. He looked up at his timer, who was carefully studying the stop watch. The timer called out his time. The swimmer hurled himself out of the pool and toward the showers, a smile on his face.

***

May 4, 1977, 15 yrs old

My name is Jim Malan and I am running for the office of "Sophomore Class President."

I seek the position of President, so that I may have the chance to help broaden the activities for the sophomore class. This past year, the sophomores as a whole were not very active in the student body. They had an activity dance early in the school year. They planned and put on a successful Soph Hop—but that was about it. This is why I'd like to be President—so that the sophomores can get involved in activities that they will benefit from and have fun doing.

The main activities that I would attempt to accomplish if elected are:

1. The Soph Hop. The Soph Hop, as most of you know, is a semi-formal dance that sophomores have in the early spring. Bids are sold as in the upper-class formal dances and the dance is held in one of the two schools. This past year the dance was held in the Carondelet inner-court. The present Soph councils from both schools worked hard and debated much over the Soph Hop. After many weeks they agreed on a band, theme, bids, etc.

This coming year the Soph council, the Vice President and myself working with the Carondelet Soph council will attempt to make the Soph Hop just as good, if not better than the past year by putting in the time and hard work that it takes to produce a successful dance.

The second main activity will be the festival ticket sales contest. This coming year there will be an inter-class competition in selling festival tickets with the winning class collecting 10% of the money they make. This money could be used for a special sophomore activity or stored for our junior year to go towards the Junior Prom. We as sophomores will have just as good of a chance as the other three classes to win the money which will really come in handy.

Thirdly, an activity that is presently in the early stages, is a combination sophomore party-picnic. This is a day when all the sophomores take a day from school and go to a park or the beach for a day. Food and transportation could be paid for from money we might earn and win from the festival sales or that we ourselves contribute, which may run about a dollar per person. The whole Soph council would help to plan and put on the event.

Furthermore, I think that I have a little more knowledge than my opponents of how the Student Council systems at De La Salle and Carondelet work because I have known the present student body president at this school, the newly elected president M _ _ _ _ H _ _ _ _, and the Sophomore class president and newly elected vice at Carondelet. Through discussion with them—I have learned how the meetings run and what takes place during them. Using this knowledge and the previous experience my running mate and I have had on student councils, I know that we could serve you well as President and Vice.

These are my ideas and proposals. Working on these and others, I know that my running mate M _ _ _ _ G _ _ _ _, and myself can add a lot to your sophomore year at D.L.S. But you do have our solemn promise—we'll try our best. So vote for Jim Malan—Sophomore Class President and M _ _ _ _ _ G _ _ _ _ _ Sophomore Vice President.

***

Jim Malan, May 31, 1977, 15 yrs old

English

Short Story Summary

"Truth and Consequences"

This story dealt with a girl. She was very plain looking and lame. She always managed to have a lot of boys around her and she constantly swore. One day, she sat next to a man about to become a priest. They started talking. She told him all about her life. Then she asked him about his life. He told her he wanted to become a priest, mainly because his mother wanted him to. The girl asked him if he really wanted to become a priest. He had to answer, "No." He really wasn't sure if he wanted to become a priest. He took the girl's hand and kept repeating, "No, No . . ." At that moment, his mother appeared. She looked so old and fragile compared to the girl. He felt a sudden upheaval within him. A major choice had to be made. His mother and the priesthood, or the girl.

This story was very emotional. I really enjoyed reading it, because it showed a person facing life and coping with major decisions. It was well-written and very easily understood. I guess I liked it so much because I know that I will soon have a lot of major decisions to make and it will be hard for me to cope with them.

***

1977

In June of 1977, I bought my first car. It was a red Pontiac convertible of the year 1968. It was in beautiful condition and it still is in good condition. There wasn't a rip in the red interior. The dashboard didn't have any cracks. The mileage was only 53,000. It had a new top. It had four new tires. It was a fantastic car.

I enjoyed it all summer. My friends and I drove everywhere with the top down. Everyone would stare at us as we drove by in the unusual car. I no longer used my parents' car. My car was much better.

Six weeks after I had gotten the car, a man walked up to me as I was sitting in it. He offered me $3500 for it. This was much more than what I had paid for it. I said no to him because I loved the car so much.

I was happy with my decision but my friends that I was stupid. In August I realized that I was going to drive the car to school every day. Although it got 15 MPG, I needed better gas mileage because school was 17 miles away from my house. I started looking for another car. After 3 days I found one. It was a beautiful 74 Toyota Celica. I couldn't let a deal like this pass. It had 30,000 miles.

It was a five speed. It had a vinyl roof and got 30 MPG.

I borrowed the money from my uncle and promised to pay it back as soon as the Pontiac was sold. I thought that the Pontiac would sell in a week but it is still for sale today. The price is $2700. My parents and my uncle are very mad that no one has bought it yet.

Now I wish I didn't buy the Celica because I am going to miss the convertible a lot in the summer. At this point I don't know what to do.

***

Binder #4

1979

Jim Malan, 1979, Junior

>Chemistry is a subject
>
>Chemistry is a terror
>
>And yet, when the bell rings,
>
>And your mind is full to the brim
>
>And your hands are trembling,
>
>You feel good
>
>You feel knowledgeable
>
>You feel adequate

Chemistry is a discussion, gasses, formulas, grades, numbers. At least to give us something to talk about or is it something to complain about? Chemistry is signing, questions, laughter and 6×10^{23}

Chemistry is something everyone looks forward to until they get there.

You're tired and stupid.

You're bleak and lazy.

You're near tears and dead.

You're depressed

***

1979, Junior

Theology & Lit

My first thought after reading this book was that May is not capable of loving. Then, after thinking for a while, I realized that I was basing my thoughts on the SS (Gestapo??) and the rest of the Germans that ran the concentration camps. The book made me develop a hatred for Germans. This struck me (fury?) because that's not like me. I usually do not prejudge people in that way. Every time a German would degrade a Jew, I felt some kind of hostility toward him and it made me really see and feel how helpless those Jews really were. They had absolutely no say in their faith. (Or should I say doom.) I just can't comprehend how one human being could be so unfeeling and degrading to another of his own kind. The Germans were definitely not capable of showing any love to anything.

I thought that the majority of the Jews were the most courageous, loving, giving, hopeful people under the gruesome circumstances that they had to endure. Of course, Elizar was the prime example of this. I don't think that I would have the courage and optimism that he had. I would have surely given up, for me as well as my father.

Many of the Jews did show some signs of being "non-loving" beings. But under such circumstances, they came out to be some of the most loving people. The one example, that sticks out in my mind is when the mass of Jews was being forced to run from one of the camps to the next, all through the night, they are in sub-zero temperatures, and icy snow. One of the boys saw that his father was weakening and falling behind in the pack. Any son would have slowed up to help his father. This boy quickened his pace and moved up further into the pack. At first, I thought this boy was sick that he would leave his own flesh and blood behind. But then I began to think of the burden that he must have carried. The thoughts that were running through his mind, I can see why he had no "love" to give.

What really struck me as a father's true love for his son was when he came back to look for his son—the son who abandoned him!!

A prime example of love was when Elizar's father died. Of course, he felt some sorrow, but not to the extent of mourning. In a sense he was glad. Not glad that his father had died, but happy and relieved that his father would not have to go through any more hell. He loved his father. He showed this love by accepting his death.

"Love" was a theme through the whole book. Of course not in the sense that we know love, but rather it was individualized. A person's love for his son, love for his wife, love for himself—even some kind of love for his enemy—and a love for his life.

***

1979, Junior

I Joined the Human Race

You could say that I was the perfect image of an introvert. I was the only person I knew. Never would I even think of introducing myself to another person. It wasn't my nature. Don't get me wrong, I didn't hate people. I really love people. It's just that I didn't want to associate with them. I felt awkward and stupid. I couldn't communicate. It was one day, two years ago, when I finally became a member of the human race.

At 7:15 a.m. I entered the BART station in Walnut Creek, bought my ticket, and proceeded up the escalator. So far, the day had been as normal as ever. Up on the platform, I took my usual seat on a bench and buried my head in the morning newspaper. I was careful not to sit by anyone so that I wouldn't be forced to engage in a conversation. I stared up from my paper and gazed at the various people on the platform. Lots were men dressed in suits and carrying briefcases. I felt that I stood out because of my dully colored over-coat, my plain white buttoned-down shirt, and my gray tweed pants. A group of ladies stood at the far end of the platform with shopping bags, constantly talking to one another about different interesting happenings.

Coming up the escalator was a "gang" of teenagers. Each male wore a black leather vest, torn jeans, and had shoulder length greasy hair. The two females also had greasy hair and large holes in their faded jeans, plus dark, ugly purses. I was quite bothered by their presence. They meandered around the platform remaining completely silent. As they passed me, I again buried my head in my newspaper. I felt sweat forming on my forehead as I prayed that they wouldn't sit next to me. Much to my relief, they passed me and waited for the train at the end of the platform.

During this traumatic experience, an elderly couple had arrived on the platform and proceeded to sit next to me. An uncomfortable state overtook me. I knew that at any moment, the man would turn and talk to me. I tried to think of how I could reply to him. How could I relate to him? A sigh of relief came over me when the train pulled into the station. I wiped the beads of sweat from my face and stood up. I literally ran to the front of the line so I could get a seat by myself. I never sat by a window, people who liked to look at the scenery would sit next to me. I got a seat at the front of the car with no window. The only problem was that my seat was facing the back of the car. Everyone else was facing me. I immediately opened my newspaper and began reading. I couldn't read knowing that all those people were constantly staring at me.

At each stop, more and more people got in the train. With each stop, I grew more and more uncomfortable. All kinds of people dressed in all manners took their seats facing me. This crazy feeling was driving me up the wall. Why was I so afraid? I was a person just like everyone else. I had feelings. Why didn't anyone else react the way I did.

The train stopped at Oakland West station. Nobody exited. Three teenagers dressed similarly to the gang that I saw at my boarding station entered the train. I pretended not to notice them. But their presence irked me. One of them came walking in my direction. He was tall and slender with tight black curly hair. The manner in which he dressed bothered me more than anything else about him. He sat next to me. My heart skipped a beat. I slowly inched away from him, pressing against the side of the train. Shivers ran up and down my trembling body. What if he talked to me? What would I say? These thoughts shot through my mind constantly.

The train had just entered the trans-bay tube. I noticed people swallowing and sticking their fingers in their ears as the pressure changed. I again pretended to read my newspaper which by this time was almost completely emulated from my clutching it. The presence of the "gangster" made the ride under the bay seem to take forever.

Suddenly, the train quickly slowed. Immediately after this it came to a stop. There were little reactions from the passengers because often the trains stopped in the tunnel so that other trains could catch up with it. After a couple minutes, I started to sweat again. The teenager crossed his legs. This startled me. I felt uneasy with each passing moment. I prayed that I wouldn't have to say anything to him.

The passengers began to get restless. This stop was an unusual one. After a couple more uneasy minutes, the conductor's voice emerged over the intercom. "Due to computer difficulties, the system will have to be shut down for at least an hour."

This statement shocked me. The other passengers became annoyed. The voice again assured us that there was no danger whatsoever. We would just have to sit quietly and wait it out.

I was terrified. Not of the fact that I was stuck on the bottom of the San Francisco Bay for an hour. I was afraid of being alone with all those people. I couldn't possibly avoid saying something to someone for an hour. There would be no way that boring, stupid me could stay sane without relating to someone for an hour. An idea dawned. I turned my head to the "gangster" and said,

"Excuse me. Since we are going to be sitting next to each other for the next hour, I thought that I'd introduce myself. My name is Robert Gordon."

He smiled as he shook my hand. And do you know what happened, he didn't even laugh at me.

Jim Malan

***

I know that I shouldn't use the musical as an excuse, but it has been a combination of that and Physics that has kept me from keeping up my Theol and Lit. I'm only on pg. 65 so I'll have to do my catching up this weekend. Then I will be able to compare the relationships.

Jim Malan, 1979

***

Jim Malan, 1979

Fantasy/Mystery

"Science Fiction" is the unforeseen of the past and the reality of the present.

What this statement means to me is that when science fiction is written, it is basically fantasy. The writer knows that what he is writing could possible, in the far distant future, become reality. He doesn't think that actually will be come true, he just knows that it may be possible. As it says in the quote: His thoughts are "unforeseen," but quite possible as for "science fiction" being the reality of the present. All one has to do is read a Sci-Fi novel written in the '30s or '40s and compare their predictions with today.

To me, it is amazing how these writers can, in minute detail, predict what is real in the future. It makes me think whether these predictions are pure luck or if society has developed to conform with the Sci-Fi novel's predictions.

***

1979, Junior

Man Becoming

In the C&O categories, there wasn't a time where I was in the minority. I was always a part of the group that contained the majority of the people. The value that probably had the nearest balance of people was "adjusting to the prevailing social norms." I believe it is valuable to adjust with society. When I heard the "rejection" views, I realized that what they had to say applied to me also. They stated that they would rather be their own person and not just be a face in the crowd. I believe this view also. This made me feel kind of awkward because I wasn't sure if I was in the right place. This made me realize that these values can take on two views and that I should decide on one without examining them both.

***

Jim's Thoughts for Songs, 1979

Steppin Out Tonite

As soon as the sun rose high in the sky.

I knew this day would be great.

My bedroom is filled with memories.

The ceiling and walls are filled.

Gone are all the happy times.

That have been so good to me.

Now's the time for happier ones.

Since you asked me, I'll tell you

Life can be happy

God knows it can be sad too.

Both physically and mentally.

God is Love

God is Life.

Life is me.

Both mentally and physically.

***

1979, Junior

Creative Writing

Love is . . .

Love is a two-way decision.

Part of me.

Part of you.

Love isn't just a provision.

We'll love each other.

'Till life is through.

Love seems to be like a turtle.

Slowly traveling.

Through time.

Love is a massive enjoyment.

Especially 'cause

You are mine

***

1979, Junior

Middle of the Road Man

We don't believe in a God per se, but we do believe that there is some being of "existence." It can't be named "God" because there is no immediate evidence, and no one is for sure knowing of a God.

We don't believe in a physical "life after death" but possibly another form of "existence" not known to us at the present. There is no real proof—but it's not ethical that this life can be as we know it.

We feel some responsibility toward helping our fellow man but not sole responsibility. They must want to help themselves—we feel that man has a certain amount of responsibility toward his fellow man.

We believe in violence in the case of self-defense or another reason—because in a sense you are preserving your own life—the primal instinct to live

Sexual actions are an individual's choice. He alone knows how he feels and he should act on these feelings, unless he has made some kind of commitment, i.e. marriage, etc.

We believe that a person should join to get guidelines and a basic understanding of God, with the understanding he can then make choices if he can believe in any form of God that he chooses.

Authority—Leadership—We do not believe in a dictatorship—all people should have a say in the way their life is run.

***

1979, Junior

American Presidents

Two limits on the president are 1—maximum of two terms on president and 2—the congress can override any decision, bill, veto, etc. Without these limits set to "restrain" the president, a certain president could take over a country that is democratic and turn it into an absolute dictatorship.

Without this set number of terms, a president could continually run for the office every four years and continually win. With a limit set on his terms, he can't do that much harm that the following president couldn't correct the damage. On the other hand, if he does well his first term and he has a good rapport with people, he will probably be elected for one more term. By continually winning election after election and remaining in office for so many years, he would have enough time and power to develop the government into his own form.

Without congressional override, the president could pass any law that he wanted, whether it was for the good of the country or for his own gain. Also, any bill that he didn't want to see made a law, and this bill (law) would greatly benefit the country, he could send it back to congress and they would not have the power to override it. Without the congress, and override, the president could make any sort of decision without going to congress first for approval. If congress played no part in the president's decisions, he could make any and all decisions and as a result become a dictator.

***

1979

J _ _ _ _,

This may seem a little awkward but I thought it would be interesting—

I'd like to know if you'd go to the Junior Prom with me? I've been meaning to ask you for a long time, but I just haven't had the chance—I thought this would be a "different" way of asking you?! I hope that you're still going to the cast party tonight.

Talk to you later,

Jim

P.S. This time I remembered to sign my name,

Jim

***

1979, Junior

Life Styles

Declaration on Sexual Ethics

It is obvious that the main trend of thought among many people (especially students my age) has something to do with sex. Many comments are made, derogatory or positive having to do with sex in one form or another. It is a topic of many discussions and/or debates (take this class!!). It's a rare occasion however, that people take this subject and closely examine it as we have just done. As you have said we are all sexed beings. It is natural for sexed beings to have sex on their minds regardless of what form of the word they are thinking about. First of all, let me give "my" definition of "sex." Sex is a part of love, for me, this includes touching, kissing, sharing, caring, forgiving, devotion, etc., all the way up to the act of intercourse itself. None of these acts are bad. I was always taught that the word "sex" was as bad as saying "shit" or "damn." Of course I don't believe that anymore. How can the deepest, and supposedly the most meaningful, expression of love be "bad?"

This is not to say that sex can't be bad. Anything can be harmful when it is gone about the wrong way. I just think that sex can be justified in more cases than "Institutions" (the Catholic Church being one of these) see it as something "justifiable." I do not think that all pre-marital sex is wrong. If two people express a deep feeling of love and devotion towards one another, sex is a fine means of expression. This love (please remember my definition of sex). If it is used purely as some sick means of cheap enjoyment or even so far as "status"—that's where I question its moral value. I'm not insinuating that the act of intercourse should be treated very lightly and "every day"—nor should it be a very sacred negative aspect. If two people feel strongly enough about each other, they should express this feeling in a "strong" manner. I agree with the Catholic Church with the fact that sexual intercourse is a means of procreation. However, this is not its foremost use. Its foremost use is that of "love." Its secondary use is procreation. I say this because I believe that the couple's openness is foremost in a relationship. Without happiness, trust, and love no relationship is complete. Children will usually exchange this type of relationship—but this type of relationship has to be established first. This brings me to birth control. I am all for birth control because I firmly believe that it is the couple's own choice as to whether they wish to have children or not. They should not have to give up sexual relations (i.e. happiness, trust, love, etc.) because of the "fear of" pregnancy. Just like they have a choice in many other aspects of their lives—so they should have a choice in the aspect of children. My views on homosexuality are quite simple. As heterosexuals have a right to express their own sexuality so I believe homosexuals are entitled to that same right. It's their choice. They wish to "seek out" and find their own form of happiness, just as the majority of the people do—let them. So far, they haven't bothered me—I feel that I have no right to condemn them, so there you have it—my views!! They don't really go along with the Catholic Church. That is in no way saying "That I don't" respect its opinions. I do. It's just that this is a very hard subject not to form your own opinions well—I have my own opinions and as of now—I like what I think.

***

Jim Malan

CHILDLESS

Money

Personal need

Selfishness

Sexual freedom

Can't handle children

1. If their friends have children

2. Friends or relatives

3. Through a job or social activity

"CHILDFULL"

Carry on name

To raise children

Have an "old fashioned" family

To give love

Satisfy oneself

It means you have to devote most of your time and energy to your kids and very little to yourself.

I think it will be very good because the care and understanding that they showed for their child will be shown toward each other.

A home with a minimum of fighting and shouting. A home where all parties express their opinions and are listened to. A home where the children are given a degree of freedom.

No they shouldn't make any special effort to pay their debt with gratitude. On the other hand, they shouldn't just take advantage of and then disregard their parents.

***

1979, Junior

From the article, I do think that Jenny and Steve communicate well. They always talk when they have problems. They confide in each other and they know each other's needs. They also know about the problems that they must face in order to keep their "young marriage" together.

I think living together aided them because as stated in the article, they learned more about each other, their shyness and different needs. Now, if they disagree, they don't get angry and they don't try to change each other.

I think that this is because they jump into marriage without really considering what it will be like. Everything goes great the first few years. Then both people start to realize the part of their life that they missed by getting married so early. They want to go back and live it and divorce seems like the good alternative.

Communication is the only thing that is going to keep a marriage together. Each person has to know how the other feels so that assumptions won't be made. The only way to accomplish this is communications.

***

1979, Junior

My Beloved Constituents of Lil Abner

We could sit here and bask in the warmth of all your friendships forever.

Though K _ _ _ _'s yelling which often "shuts us up," and P _ _ _ 's endless energy, combined with D _ _ _ 's will to get things done, we've managed to stick together and pull off a knee slapping, mouth watering, hand clapping show.

We've enjoyed every minute of it. From C _ _ _'s tight pants, butt swayin' walk, to Moonbeams beauty. But we are sincere in saying that we truly enjoyed working with every single one of you. Through the good and the bad. We have managed to pull through all of our drawbacks. We truly look forward to next year's show and seeing all of you again. For all of you who won't be back we really wish our love for all of you seniors like J _ _ _ and F _ _ _ who have made us laugh since our freshman year. You have cheered us up during bad times, so that you once again for your support. Forget the $2.00 wedding—let's give them a hundred dollars.

HA HA

***

1979, Junior

Lifestyles

For a marriage unit to develop, there must, of course, be love. Also, mutual understanding, trust and respect. You must be able to fulfill the other's need and be flexible to their needs.

It is more important that they respect and understand each other, because they can then realize why the other person thinks like he does and on what facts he bases his decisions. Then they can better communicate their opinions on other topics.

If a person is afraid to adopt a child of another race because of what people think, this is due to ignorance. People should realize that the love the parents have for the child overcomes all fears that they would have over the adoption. What they feel should overcome what people feel about them.

***

1979, Junior

To the problems of abortion

This article was interesting the way that it showed that each possible "answer" to the abortion problem, developed many more new problems that have to be dealt with.

I can see how hard it is to classify abortion as "right" or "wrong." Society isn't advanced enough to handle such a sophisticated and intricate problem as this one. Perhaps, in time an agreed-on solution will be found.

***

May 18, 1979

Mathew 27-28

Man Becoming

My passage was the familiar tale concerning the crucifixion and resurrection of Jesus. It is very obvious that at this point in Jesus' life most of his actions are for the benefit of mankind, and not so much for himself. Jesus doesn't speak in his defense when confronted by Pilate.

He rather let the people make false accusations about him. This obviously shows that Jesus is not acting for himself or else he would speak in his own favor. Likewise, he also remains silent when the guards taunt him. "Save yourself, save yourself" and yet Jesus as magnificent and powerful as he is remains silent and humble and takes all this.

His actions here display certain guidelines by which we should govern our own actions. Humility and humbleness throughout Jesus' entire life, he constantly displays his humility. He never exalts himself or praises himself for all the good that he accomplishes. He remains humble. This is a message of how we are to act. Nobody likes a bragger. Many times I find myself telling people about all the good that I have done. Afterward, when I think about it, I feel stupid and ashamed.

Of course proves himself as the son of God three days later. But again, the actual action of the resurrection is for the benefit of others. (This act could be and is sometimes looked at not as benefitting Jesus himself. He is proving himself and getting back at the people for all the accusations they convicted him of.) After the resurrection, he baptizes the disciples and for the benefit of the people (again) he instructs them to go out into the world, baptizing, and tell all men about everything he has commanded. Again—for the benefit of the people—so they can have a chance at everlasting life.

Since there were no parables in my passage, there were no real "sudden meanings" that I could "dig up." Most of what was said was pure fact. The one thing that is evident from the reading is that all Jesus' actions were for the benefit of other people and not Jesus alone.

***

Jim Malan

Life-Styles

Respond briefly to the following in short paragraphs

Would you consider a teenage marriage? Why? Why not?

At this point I would say no! I plan to go to college and then on to Med School and that is going to be enough responsibility in itself.

What outside influences might be involved in your decision making on this question?

As stated above—schooling. I want to be stable and set on myself and my life when I get married.

Does any of the above-mentioned make you feel pressured in this matter?

Yes, but the pressure is self-imposed. It's what I want to do. There is no pressure from an outside source.

How could a teen marriage be valuable in some ways? Harmful?

Valuable—if the two people are level-headed and really care for each other—the marriage could work out fine. Harmful—As I see it, one of the main reasons a teenage marriage can be harmful is lack of money. Teenagers are less experienced in the way of a job. Thus it is harder for them to earn the needed money to lead the kind of life that they are used to.

***

1979, Junior

Daily Log

02/28/79

Well, today I found out I made "West Side Story." I was cast as a shark. This doesn't bother me. I went to the theater to tell them that I'd do the part. I talked to the girl I know that works in the box office. She told me that the stage version of "WSS" isn't really like the television movie. She said sharks do very little in the stage version. I still wasn't very mad because what little the shark did do was still good, dancing in a couple big numbers. But then, she told me that the director was going to bring in his own dancers. I wasn't going to get to dance. I was just going to be a chorus member. I decided here that the show wasn't worth my time.

I thought I was disappointed and didn't want to do the show, I rejected the part.

***

Daily Log

Feb. 29, 1979

Opening Nite!! For Guys & Dolls

I'm really excited, especially after the show we put on for the student matinee.

It was great!! The show really went off well. I'm not past the point of being tired, but God I am. I'm excited. The house is almost sold out and my family and friends are coming. I know it will be good.

Opening nights are always good.

There's a certain electricity that flows through each cast member. This makes us put on a great show. I wish these ten hours would pass faster.

***

1979, Junior

April 24, 1979

Man Becoming

I wasn't too surprised with my test results. The fields that I am interested in appeared in my high interest and average interest columns. One thing that I did notice from the test was that there are many careers that I never even thought of that interest me. I could see myself in each one of those jobs. I'm seriously thinking about entering the field of medicine.

The things that are holding me back are the competitiveness and the many years of studying. Seeing these other career choices has made me seriously thing about other possible career alternatives.

***

Man Becoming

Jim Malan, April 27, 1979

The Tendencies of Man

This song tells about the fantasy that every man has; a fantasy to do with a goal he has set for himself. "The world can't erase his fantasy, no matter how tough life may become."

"Bigshot" portrays how a man can show-off to the point that he "gets in trouble." He becomes disliked by his peers. Man has this problem in this day. He has to know about everything. He shows off to gain attention. He focuses the spotlight on himself, all for self-recognition.

"Superman" portrays man as a fantasy figure, the perfect man. He is not a bird or a plane, but a special "man," able to accomplish things that others cannot.

In "Honesty," the fact is brought out that many men are untruthful towards their fellow man. But for me to survive peacefully together, they need to be openly honest with each other.

"I won't last a day without you," could portray a man entering new, unfamiliar situations: encountering many strange people. Man needs someone; some close friend to turn to for help, his "smallest dreams to come true."

"Rainy days and Mondays" displays this feeling by showing that men sometimes want to quit and give up. They sometimes feel that their life is leading them nowhere.

"My life" is a powerful song that shows that men want to and in fact deserve to lead their own lives. They don't need help from others. Let the others "go ahead with their own lives and leave him alone."

"Take it to the limit" again deals with dreaming. Men are constantly dreaming of what they want their life to turn out like. Given the right opportunities, a man can fulfill his dreams.

"Just show man a sign" and he'll take his dreams to the limit . . . and fulfill it.

"Where do I go from here" displays man's confusion that he often possesses. He asks questions and relies on other men to answer them.

"If" is a unique example of a man's dreams to be in two places at one time. To be with a special friend forever. To have the world end. To "fly away."

Man can be seen in many different ways. Through fantasy, depression, dreams, confusion and countless others, man is never alike in any two ways. He is constantly changing his attitude and beliefs, and as a result, he is constantly changing the life that he lives.

***

Science and Society

Jim Malan, May 19, 1979

Can technology solve the abortion dilemma?

Through many technological breakthroughs, such as amniocentesis, a woman can find out whether or not her baby has a genetic defect, is diseased or what sex it is. Many women use this test as a basis for their making a decision on whether to have an abortion or not. Most women agree that abortion is wrong, but again whether to have an abortion or not is the woman's decision and only her decision. These women are also opposed to a Constitutional Amendment which prohibits abortion.

Many women are hoping to see a new medical breakthrough by which if the woman desires not to have the baby, she can have it removed from her body and allow it to live in an artificially constructed uterus without "killing" it. This method, of course, brings up many moral and ethical problems.

Who would have custody of the child? Could a mother reclaim her child? Who assumes financial responsibility for the child, etc.?

Personally—I think there are no definite answers to the problems of abortion.

***

Jim Malan, May 29, 1979

Man Becoming

Other people might want to deprive me of my own pleasure for a number of reasons that are outstanding to them, but not relevant to me.

I sometimes feel that my parents deprive me of going out or doing something that I want to do, because they feel some sort of jealousy. That is, they don't have the time I have to enjoy themselves as much as they like to. The church depriving me of enjoyment isn't a "direct depriving" as with my parents. The church has to set up a set of standards. These standards must apply to all people. What I feel is that the church is depriving me of and not necessarily what the next person feels, and so on. I don't see the church as depriving me of my enjoyment now, maybe later in life this view may change.

Because I have always obeyed the law and stayed with social trends, I have never looked upon society as depriving me of enjoyment. I don't see the laws and social norms as something set up to deprive people. I see them as a set of rules by which people should govern their actions. I can see though, how people who break these laws and have to suffer the consequences may see the laws as depriving them of their enjoyment. This is different because these people "know how they will be deprived" before they complete the action.

***

11/21/79 10:24 AM

Dear Jim (my good friend),

Well, I know that you had a fantastic time on your Senior Retreat and I know how much you'd love to stay some more but it has to end sometime. I could tell some important things about you just from watching you. You met a few new people; you developed some closer relationships; you "assessed" the value of other relationships; you looked and found some good in everyone on retreat.

When you go back, and particularly over Christmas, try not to lose the wonderful feeling of contentment which you are feeling this minute. Try to share this feeling with your friends and especially your family. And promise me that you'll try something. Always look for the good in every person.

I'm not saying that you shouldn't dislike someone, but even if there is a certain person that bugs you, treat them nice. Be true to your friends. Let them know that they are your friends and that they care. Be true to your family and finally be true to God.

He knows all.

He loves you

Love him

Love Jim

***

Jim Malan

154 Haven Hill Ct

Danville, CA 84526

(415) 837-4091

Birth date: April 27, 1962

Age: 16 years old

Height 6'1" Weight 157

A junior at De La Salle High School in Concord. Involved in various dramatic, musical and dance productions. An active member of various clubs and holds a position on the student council.

Member of the International Thespian Society

Grade point average 3.6

Past stage productions

School productions

-- "Two Gentlemen of Verona" March, 1977 "Speed"/dancer

-- "Our Town" November, 1976 "Wally Webb"

-- "The Diary of Anne Frank" November 1977 Stage Manager

-- "My Fair Lady" March 1978 "Harry"/dancer/understudy for "Freddy E. Hill"

-- "Godspell" July, 1978 "Jeffrey"

-- "Lil Abner" to be staged March 1979 "Marryin' Sam"/dancer/understudy to Lil Abner

Community productions

-- Miss Walnut Creek Pageant 1977. August, 1977 Pageant singer and dancer

-- Miss Walnut Creek Pageant 1978. August, 1978 Pageant singer and dancer

-- "Peter Pan" December 1978. Civic Arts Young Repertory. "Indian"/dancer

Past singing experience

-- Grammar school choir, 4 years

-- Church folk group, 2 years

-- De La Salle Men's Chorus, 2 years

Past music experience

-- Organist for 11 years

-- School organist in grammar school

-- Church organist for 5 years

-- Plans for the future are to graduate from high school and major in medicine, perform in Musical Theater.

***

Jim Malan

154 Haven Hill Ct

Danville, CA 84526

(415) 837-4091

11/26/79

OCCUPATIONAL GOAL: Would like to start out as a teller and possible work up to a position in NCR, New Accounts, or Accounts Reconcilement. Salary desired: $600.00/mo.

EDUCATION: De La Salle High School, Winton Dr. Concord, CA

Beneficial subjects: Algebra I & II, Geometry, Trigonometry

Grade point average: 3.7

WORK HISTORY:

5/7/79 – 9/9/79 Bank of America NT&SA

1307 N. Broadway Walnut Creek, CA 94596

Positions: Stock manager, check filer, statements

Salary: $600.00/mo.

6/78 and continuing St. Anne's Catholic Church

Rossmoor Pkwy Walnut Creek, CA 94596

Position: Church organist

Salary: $50.00/mo.

6/78 – 8/78 Swimming instructor

6/79 – 8/79 Worked out of home

Salary: $300.00/mo.

6/77 – 9/79 Contra Costa Times

Walnut Creek, CA 94596

Position: Paper carrier

Salary: $40.00/mo.

SCHOOL AND EXTRA-CURRICULAR ACTIVITIES:

-- Sophomore Class President, 1 year

-- Student Council, 2 years

-- Rally Club, 2 years

-- Company, 4 years

-- Swim Team, 1 year

-- Honor Roll, 4 years

PERSONAL DATA:

Date of birth: 4/27/62 17 yrs. old

Single

Height: 6'2" Weight: 160 lbs.

HOBBIES:

Swimming, musical theater, day trips (on weekends of course)

***

1979, Junior

    THANKSGIVING

    The sweet smells of berries and turkey and bread

    Search for the people whose mouths shall be fed.

    For inside the kitchen my mother and sis

    Create a masterpiece, sealed with a kiss.

    The snow on the ground and the fire in the den

    Create a feeling that is loved by all men.

    The family's at home all together as one

    And Grandma and Grandpa join in on the fun.

    The table is set with the best china ware.

    With flowers and laces and fruit from the fair.

    We all take our places and fold our hands tight.

    We thank God for all as we take our first bite.

When dinner is through and everyone's tired

The family sits down to talk by the fire.

This joy should be shared with all who are living,

'Cause the happiest of times is the time of thanksgiving.

James Malan

November 1979

***

Oklahoma, 1979

"Oklahoma" a Fresh Delight

By Abel Kessler

Take a break from the tube and go see real live people perform "Oklahoma," presented at the Willows Theater by Concord Community Arts.

A standing ovation at the finale was the demonstrated opinion of the opening night audience last Friday. It was deserved, for the production was delightful with fine singing and played with a freshness and enthusiasm that was contagious.

"Oklahoma," of course, is in the musical Hall of Fame. Going into its fourth decade, it surprises by its continued appeal. The story of how romances were conducted before Oklahoma became a state may contrast with modern methods—but that, perhaps, is why it is so charming.

From the opening, when Curly sings "Oh, What a Beautiful Day," the tone is set for the pleasantness that prevails throughout. Maybe the upbeat theme makes the musical all the more attractive in today's worrisome world, just as it did when it was first seen during World War II.

Jody Smith Benecke and Jeffrey Carney carried the principal boy-girl roles of Laurey and Curly with pleasing professionalism and attractive trained voices. Their handsome appearances made the characters convincing. The lady added the proper dramatic mixture to her femininity while her suitor supplied the necessary macho ingredient.

The unsympathetic role of Jud Fry, the villain, was skillfully handled by Cliff Ballou. The audience hated Jud but they loved Ballou. His vocal interpretation was just right for the part—as was his bulk.

The seasoned singers were joined by a pixie-like youngster with a sense of comedy who may well be a new talent on the way up. She is Kimberly Mickey, a Northgate High senior, who romped through the Ado Annie role as though it was a fun day away from school.

There is no denying that Ado Annie's song, "I Can't Say No," is a classic comic composition. But only recently on TV, superstar Carol Burnett worked over the same song and, to this viewer, it didn't come out as well as Mickey's performance. (In fairness, the role calls for a chick, not a veteran.)

The entire cast acted as if they were enjoying themselves and that carried across to the audience which filled every seat and even stood at the rear of the house. The longest applause came with almost all the performers onstage in the final scene. It was the outdoor party and everyone cavorted as if they were having a ball.

As Aunt Eller, Ann Bruno competently kept the story line progressing. The difficult comic relief peddler was carried by Rick Bruno. Offstage, the Brunos take care of their eight children.

Chris Constantouros, whose credits show an excellent dancing career, displayed he can also sing in "The Farmer and the Cowman" number.

James Malan as Will Parker was exactly the young man you would expect to finally win Ado Annie. Carolyn Kraetch made the most of her tiny Granny part and evoked laughter with he gestures.

The ballet alter-egos of the hero and heroine were danced with spirit by Kimberly A. Marshall and Robert Hand. Diane Alexander and Pill Pidanick won good marks in their supporting parts.

Director David Gerrard must be a magician. Somehow he blended people ranging from students to full careerists into a cast that worked well.

If you have not been to the Willows Theater treat yourself to a visit. It is intimate—only 198 seats—a small gem that is far more suited for real theater than many summer stock places.

Presented by the Concord Community Arts, "Oklahoma" is scheduled through Nov. 10. Performances are listed for every Friday and Saturday at 8 p.m. There are also four Sunday and three Thursday dates. Check the box office in The Willows Shopping Center or call 798-6525 or 671-3065. Students under 17 and seniors of 55 received reduced rates.

***

James Malan (Will Parker)

Jim, a senior at De La Salle High School, plans to major in pre-med in college while continuing his participation in theatre. His recent roles include Marryin' Same in "Li'l Abner," Wally Webb in "Our Town," Speed in "Two Gentlemen of Verona," Harry in "My Fair Lady," and Jeffry in "Godspell." Jim has been involved with Civic Arts Young Repertory productions and has appeared as a singer and dancer in the past three Miss Walnut Creek pageants. The Danville resident enjoys singing, dancing, swimming, and going to the beach, and last summer worked at Bank of America, taught swimming lessons, and played the organ at church.

***

Willows Theatre hosts "Oklahoma"

Two Danville men star in the Concord Community Arts production of "Oklahoma," now running at the Willows Theatre in Concord through Nov. 10. They are (left Cliff Ballou, who plays the menacing hired hand, Jud, and James Malan, who plays Will Parker, suitor of Ado Annie, the girl who "Can't Say No." The show runs every Friday and Saturday evening at 8 p.m. as well as Sundays, Oct. 21 and 28 at 2 p.m. and this Sunday and next as well as Nov 4 at 7 p.m. It will also play Thursdays Oct. 18 and Nov. 1 and 8, at 8 p.m. Very limited tickets are available, interested persons should call 798-6525 or stop by the Willows Theatre Box Office, 1975 Diamond Boulevard, Concord, open noon to 6 p.m. Tuesday through Friday and noon to 4 p.m. Saturday and Sunday.

***

1979, Junior

Life

Life is a journey and a reward

Entertainment,

Information.

Look what's new!

Show respect.

And tomorrow- Use philosophy. Be comfortable.

Life begins when death occurs.

Life begins when occurs death.

Life begins death when occurs.

Life begins . . . Death occurs when.

Life beings occurs when death.

Life when death begins, occurs.

Life when occurs, begins death.

Life when occurs, death begins.

Life, when begins, occurs death.

Life, death occurs, - begins when.

Life death-when occurs began.

Life occurs when death begins.

Life occurs when begins death.

James Malan

***

1979, Junior

Reflections on life After Life

by Raymond A. Moody M.D.

This book was not a story parse but rather a large account of many case histories. The book dealt with investigation of an extraordinary phenomenon survival of life after bodily death.

The subject was approached in a very interesting way. The author in a way broke the book down into categories such as: new elements, judgment, suicide reactions from the ministry, and historical examples. This breaking down process made the book much easier to understand.

On the whole, the book was nothing more than interviews, with people who had allegedly died and then returned to life. All of these people had experiences during their death. Many of the experiences were very similar. Many varied according to the type of death they had undergone.

Although the little details of these peoples' experiences differed, they all spoke of one or two aspects that were quite common: Each person who had "died," no matter how long it was that they were "dead," spoke of seeing themselves in another existence. These existences varied from tunnels, to pits, to soaring through a vacuum. Nevertheless, they all saw themselves as if they were looking at another person. Also, each person spoke of "light." Many of the people saw a single bright light which they followed. Others found themselves surrounded by a fantastic amazing white array of light. In every case, every person thought of this light as the presence of some other being. Many of them cannot specify "who" this being was. Others are sure that it was God.

Another aspect of death that was quite common among the people interviewed was the "feeling" that each one had after returning to life. They all came to believe that the ability to love others and the accumulation of knowledge were the two most important goals to seek in life.

When asked to define this "love and knowledge," the people answered that there are no human words to describe how they came about these thoughts.

On the whole, it was very difficult for the interviewees to describe their accounts. The reason for this as each one stated, was the fact that the English language itself was a major hindrance. Many of them, as they were trying to detail their experience, kept reminding the author that their account was very vague and capsulized compared to their actual experience. No words could describe the situation that they found themselves. Their accounts were only mere representations of what it was really like. One man describes how he felt by saying-

"Take everything that I have told you about, the light, the presence of justice, this "knowing all" feeling, the floating, the contentment, take all these and multiply them by infinity squared. Then maybe you will have the faintest idea of what I have experienced."

In Jim's words

***

1977

1978

1979

Binder #5

1980

"It's My Life"

Jim Malan

<u>James John Malan</u>

    born April 27, 1962

    born to a new life August, 24, 1980

Dear God,

Eighteen years ago you sent this world, this community, and in particular, a family, the Malans, a delightful new gift, JIMMY.

He is a gift that will remain forever with us. We are deeply grateful.

We have learned something else about your "Gift-Giving." You really do love us very much. Jimmy is a proof of your love.

He gave himself to us in so many ways, and how he has given himself to you because you need him.

It helps us to remember Jesus did this and continues His "Gift-Giving" each day.

We are thankful to you God because Jimmy was one of the best examples of Jesus that we know. Until we join Jimmy and Jesus in the Resurrected LIFE, be with us each day.

Amen/Alleluia

***

    A GRAVE MISUNDERSTANDING

    The rose grew steadily

    it's beginning—a mere simple bud—

    and flourished

    the sun reached with care

    to caress

    other flowers surrounded soon thereafter, soil gave it strength and wind cooled its delicate petals

whenever there was anger, heat, frustration,

or fear

You ask how to describe

this young unfolding life—

an impossibility, be assured

a talented rose,

with a stem that changed so day to day

and leaves that withered,

yet never died

Truly a remarkable sight

and pleasing to the eye

perhaps, a bit of heaven here on earth?

perhaps . . .

No secrets held this rose unknown,

for all could see

a striving, breathing, specialness,

that touched so many

for every living, growing thing around

was colorful

Enjoying jovial lives

and content

especially in the light

of their radiant friend

And once—but once a dark day fell

as did that cold morn

when Puff the magic dragon saw his last,

and alike the land of Honalee

a tear was shed

and another

a chunk of sky turned gray

and many

many

misunderstanding

All the while the cool wind

caressed the garden filled with living things

the breeze was felt

yet,

no one understood

Somewhere

still the rose lives on,

probably hand in hand

with the cool wind

understand?

there's one that never will

9/1980

***

It takes a special person to be able to touch so many individuals in such a short time, and in such a positive way. Jim Malan was that special person. He clearly shined in each of his many roles. He sparkled as student, brother, entertainer, and friend.

In the theatre, Jim was a true professional. He brought life and movement to a silent character in a black and white script, whether it be Speed, Friend of Valentine, Harry, Doolittle's sidekick, Marryin' Sam, or Nicely-Nicely Johnson; I feel honored to have been given the opportunity to work with such a master craftsman.

Good friends and slight acquaintances knew of Jim's caring nature. He responded to his friends beyond the call of duty. He was gentle and kind, quite different than any other man of eighteen, yet the same. Jim Malan was full of hope and he always searched for the light at the end of the tunnel, that heaven "over the rainbow" Jim—I think you found it.

Ann Lewis

1/28/81

***

THE COVER

Leslie Carrasa's gift to the Malan family at the time of Jim's rebirth to another life. Accompanying her drawing was this expression of her feelings.

> "With all my love
>
> and all my heart,
>
> this, is for you
>
> in honor of your new start.
>
> Your caring eyes and fabulous grin
>
> has captured us all deep within.
>
> You look upon us as we look up to you
>
> and each is born into something new.
>
> With all my love, and all my heart,
>
> Les'"
>
> ***

PROMISE YOURSELF

PROMISE yourself to be so strong that nothing can disturb your peace of mind. To talk health, happiness and prosperity to every person you meet. To make all your friends feel that there is something in them. To look at the sunny side of everything and make your optimism come true. To think only of the best, to work only for the best and expect only the best. To be just as enthusiastic about the success of others as you are about your own. To forget the mistakes of the past and press on to the greater achievements of the future. To wear a cheerful countenance at all times and give every living creature you meet a smile. To give so much time to the improvement of yourself that you have no time to criticize others. To be too large for worry, too noble for anger, too strong for fear and too happy to permit the presence of trouble.

Christian D. Larsen proclaims a perfect creed to emulate. As we enter this brand New Year I will try to practice his philosophy on a daily basis.

By Jim (found in his papers)

***

One Night I Had a Dream . . .

I dreamed I was walking along the beach with The Lord, and across the sky flashed scenes from my life. For each scene I noticed two sets of footprints in the sand, one belong to me, the other to The Lord. When the last scene of my life flashed before us I looked back at the footprints in the sand. I noticed that many times along the path of my life, there was only one set of footprints. I also noticed that it happened at the very lowest and saddest times in my life. I questioned The Lord about it, "Lord, you said that once I decided to follow you, you would walk with me all the way, but I have noticed that during the most troublesome times in my life, there is only one set of footprints. I don't understand why in times when I needed you most, you would leave." The Lord replied, "My precious child, I would never leave you during your times of trial and suffering. When you see only one set of footprints, it was then that I carried you."

Author unknown

March, 1979

A copy in all Jim's papers

***

    Right now I'm

    In a rut

    That I can't get out of.

I'm walking in a ditch

Two feet wide

And so deep

You can barely see

The blue sky

And sunshine overhead.

And the sides around

Are so completely

Perpendicular

To the bottom

That you can't get out

No matter how much

You want to.

So

I simply continue

Down the narrow way

That is open,

Hoping

It might widen

A little

To let in more air.

Right now I can't see

Where they say

The ditch opens out

Into meadowland and flowers.

And I've about forgotten

What meadowland looks like.

Besides,

I've never been

In this ditch before

And how do I know

That it doesn't go

Down

Inside the ground

Instead of out

Into green meadowland?

My only hope

Is what is whispered

On a wisp of breeze

From up where the sky is.

But that doesn't help

Very much.

I feel hot and sticky

And pressed in

And it's getting stuffy—

Then the Lord

Whispers to me

Like a cool, cool breath

Of fresh air:

"Do you know

That I have been

In a pathway

Deep and narrow

Like this?

Do you remember

That I found it

So hard,

That there were

Sweat-drops of blood?

Do you remember

That all my friends

Forsook me

And I, too, was

Alone?

And then God had to

Turn his face away, too.

Don't you know

That I am with you

And that I go before you

Even in this ditch?

I still love you.

You are very precious

To me.

Can't you just

Trust me

Now?"

"Yes, Lord

I will, Lord

Forever and ever.

And,

You know,

I think I can smell the meadowland!"

(In Jim's papers)

***

APPLAUSE!

** What is it that we're living for?

Applause, Applause,

Nothing I know brings on the glow,

Like sweet applause.

You're thinking you're through,

That nobody cares, then suddenly you hear it starting!

And somehow you're in charge again, and it's a ball,

Trumpets sing, Life seems to swing and you're the king of it all, 'cause

Repeat**

You're catching the flu, you're bank account's bare.

You're lonely and blue, Then you, hear it!

And all at once you know again, what life is for,

Cares disappear, Soon as you hear, that happy audience roar

'Cause you've had a taste of the sound that says

Love

Applause, Applause, Applause!

(In Jim's papers)

***

I've Got A Name

Like the pine trees lining the winding road

I've got a name, I've got a name.

Like a singing bird and the croaking toad

I've got a name, I've got a name

And I carry it with me like my Daddy did

But I'm living the dream that he can't hear

Moving me down the highway, rolling me down the highway

Moving ahead so life won't pass me by

Like a north wind whistling down the sky

I've got a song, I've got a song

Like the whisper will and the baby's cry

I've got a song, I've got a song.

And I carry it with me and I sing it loud

If it gets me nowhere, I'll go there proud.

Moving me down the highway, rolling me down the highway

Moving ahead so life won't pass me by.

And I'm gonna go there free

Like the fool I am and I'll always be

I've got a dream, I've got a dream

They can change their minds, but they can't change me

I've got a dream, I've got a dream

I know I could share it if you want me to

If you're going my way, I'll go with you

Moving me down the highway, rolling me down the highway

Moving ahead so life won't pass me by.

(In Jim's papers)

***

Jim Malan, 1980

<u>HE WAS MY BROTHER</u>

Brother to us all,

Always there when you needed him,

Never let you fall.

We were the lucky ones,

He touched our live,

Someone who heard us,

He saw through our eyes.

The laughter and loving,

The times that we shared,

You don't see till it's over,

How much you really cared.

Life is a mystery,

Full of surprises,

Destiny is chosen,

It could happen anytime.

James Malan, May 31, 1980

Written for Brother Allen, who had a rafting accident May 24, 1980

***

Mothers . . .

The thing to remember about mothers is

They're women.

A boy has to keep this in mind,

They're full to the brim with problems

Worrying all the time.

A bundle of loads on their shoulders

They always have to look nice,

In the kitchen cooking dinner;

Her favorite is chicken and rice.

In the morning she wakes you up to humming

At night she sings you to sleep.

But sometimes she fills up with anger,

And from me she hears not a peep.

But she always seems to be friendly

She always seems to like.

I remember one day last summer

When she bought me my ten speed bike.

But remember, mothers are human

They're sometimes a pain in the rear,

But we always seem to forgive her

And then she calls you "dear"

On those occasions when she blows up

We try to quiet her down.

Mothers try their hardest

And not ever once do they frown.

James Malan "80"

***

Jim Malan, 1980

Man Becoming

For the first ten minutes of this exercise, I wasn't sure what I was expected to do. As people started walking around and "communicating" I felt more relaxed, but I still felt a little stupid. I only "stuck by" the people who I knew. I thought that the act of drawing on the boards was a good idea. It got many people to express their ideas in their own way. That was the main ice-breaker for me. I'm disappointed that I didn't relate to other people whom I didn't really know. This exercise did help me find out about other people in the way that I saw which people were most outgoing and which people mostly stuck to themselves. Most people seemed to have smiles on their faces. This told me that this exercise was profitable by making people "open up" and "relate" to one another.

**

Jim Malan, 1980

"Winners and Losers"

From Born to Win:

Gestalt Experiments

Authenticity (true) to myself form of psychology therapy

Not important

Others

Events

Race, etc.

Religion

How I handle me at present is important

***

James J. Malan, 1980

A ship is safe in the protection of a harbor, but is that what a ship is constructed for? (a poster)

I recently read this quote on a poster during my Senior Retreat. This quote struck me and made me think for a few moments. I tried picturing myself as a ship—docked in a harbor, waiting to be set a sail on the risky seas. This describes me. I want to sail—to take risks—to accomplish what I've been built for.

I graduated from a small Catholic grammar school in Danville, CA. Like most 8th grade graduates, I was anxiously anticipating high school. I wanted to get involved—really involved in many activities that weren't offered in grade school. I had some experience during grade school. I tried to get involved as much as I could—I worked the audio visual equipment, served on the student council, was yearbook photographer, participated in the school choir folk group, wrote a school play. I always was a seeker for contests—I entered poetry, essays, math, science, all types of contests. I ran track and field for 3 yrs. I took ballroom dance classes. I never wanted to stop. I feel wasted when I am not doing something. I was still working hard, kept up my grades and ranked 4th in my graduating class of 44.

At this time, my dream was to become an actor and singer. I was always impressed and envious of motion picture stars. I wanted to be just like them.

While I was active in school, I kept even more busy by swimming on a rec. team for 5 years and playing the organ since the 1st grade, and singing in my church folk group and participating in Cub Scouts and Boy Scouts.

I was accepted at De La Salle High School in Concord. This was 17 miles away from my home in Danville. High school was a wonderfully new and exciting experience for me, and any fear or apprehension about high school that I had quickly disappeared. The first thing I did in high school was to get involved. To satisfy my dream, I tried out for the school's drama, "Our Town" and made it. It was this show that I made most of my friends. I also participated in the school's swim team, as well as the local AAU Spartan swim team. My day was very fast paced, but that was what I wanted.

For the first three months of my freshman year I woke up at 4:00 AM for my paper route and so I could get to school for the 5:30 AM practices and then to class at 7:30 AM until 2:30 PM. Play rehearsal from 3 to 5 PM, then I was dropped off at the local pool for AAU swim practice at 6 PM. Practice ran until 8 PM.

I'd be home for my late dinner by 8:30 PM. Did my homework and tried to be in bed by 10:30 PM and after 3 months it got tiring—with closing nigh of "Our Town" and the culmination of the school swim season, I made a choice.

I decided to end AAU swimming and concentrate on my school work and school activities. I got a lead in the musical "Two Gents." I was a member of the Rally Club and after the musical I worked on various crews for the school comedy. On weekends I would play the organ at church and sing in the folk group. At the academic awards night in June I received awards in English, Social Studies and Spanish.

That summer—I rejoined swim team, sang and danced in the "Miss Walnut Creek Pageant," and moped my paper route.

After what seemed a great year Sept. came and with that, the start of my soph year.

I decided to run for a class office for that year. Well, I ran for soph class president and won. My involvement in school had really paid off. After what seemed a year, Sept. came. I was most excited because I was soph class president. I was associate director for the drama "Diary of Anne Frank." I was in the musical MFL. Between rehearsals, school and student council meetings I managed to find time for Rally Club, school choir and the school Lit committee and to work backstage on the comedy "Charley's Aunt."

I ended my soph year as a member of the International Thes.Soc. and an award in English.

The following summer was much the same as the previous, but even more active—I got a job at a local church playing the organ. I also started my own business teaching swim lessons in my backyard. With the money from these 2 jobs and my paper route I managed to save enough money to buy myself a moped. My parents paid for half and I paid them back monthly.

I also was in "Godspell" at my school's campus—and in everything else tied up with the "Miss WC" rehearsals.

The 2nd HS summer flew by and right behind it was my junior year.

I still kept on my participation in the student council, the Lit committee and Rally Club. I worked in a crew for the drama "Lil Abner" and I had a lead.

I worked on a crew for the comedy "The Odd Couple."

Outside of school, I still had my job as an organist. I was in a musical "Peter Pan."

In May I got a job at Bank of America after school each day.

I ended my junior year with awards in Spanish 3, Chemistry, English and History.

I kept my job at the bank working 6 hours a day—I taught swim lessons 3 hours a day—and still kept my route and organ job. I also kept up my "Miss WC" tradition.

Right before the start of my senior year—I got a lead in the community show of Oklahoma. I worked on a crew for the drama. Two weeks ago—I took a leave from my bank job so I could try out for the school musical "Guys and Dolls." I just got off my senior retreat on which I helped organize and participate in the services.

The rest of my senior year promises as much activity. I plan to work on the other drama productions.

I'm going to reopen my job at the bank in March. I plan to try out for school valedictorian.

I am just now beginning to help organize graduation.

Jim Malan

<u>Freshman – School</u>

Our Town

Two Gents

Swim team

Choir

Rally Club

"Harry"—crew company

Awards

Medal for swim

Certificate for Spanish

English

<u>Community</u>

Swim team AAU

Church FG, organ

Paper route

Miss W Creek

<u>Sophomore - school</u>

Soph class pres.

Student Body Council

My Fair Lady

Rally Club

Diary of Anne Frank (assist director)

Charley's Aunt—The Crew

School Lit Committee

Godspell – S.S.

Company

Awards—Thespian

English

<u>Community</u>

Church FG, organ

Job – organ

Swim lessons

AAU

Miss WC

Moped

<u>Junior – School</u>

Student Body Rep

Spoon River (crew)

Lil Abner

Odd Couple (crew)

School Lit

Rally Club

Company Thespian

Awards – Spanish 3, Chemistry

Community

Peter Pan

Organist

B of A

Swim lessons

Miss W Creek

Car

Senior – school

Rebecca (crew)

Guys and Dolls

Rally Club

Lit Comm on Retreat

Thespian

Planning

Try out for Wal.

2 shows

Work

S.L. Church

Community

Oklahoma CCA

B of A

Swim lessons

Organ

***

Jim Malan

154 Haven Hill Ct

Danville, CA 84526

(415) 837-4091

Birth date: April 27, 1962

Age: 16 years old

Height 6'1" Weight 157

A junior at De La Salle High School in Concord. Involved in various dramatic, musical and dance productions. An active member of various clubs and holds a position on the student council.

Member of the International Thespian Society

Grade point average 3.6

Past stage productions

School productions

-- "Two Gentlemen of Verona" March, 1977 "Speed"/dancer

-- "Our Town" November, 1976 "Wally Webb"

-- "The Diary of Anne Frank" November 1977 Stage Manager

-- "My Fair Lady" March 1978 "Harry"/dancer/understudy for "Freddy E. Hill"

-- "Godspell" July, 1978 "Jeffrey"

-- "Lil Abner" to be staged March 1979 "Marryin' Sam"/dancer/understudy to Lil Abner

Community productions

-- Miss Walnut Creek Pageant 1977. August, 1977 Pageant singer and dancer

-- Miss Walnut Creek Pageant 1978. August, 1978 Pageant singer and dancer

-- "Peter Pan" December 1978. Civic Arts Young Repertory. "Indian"/dancer

Past singing experience

-- Grammar school choir, 4 years

-- Church folk group, 2 years

-- De La Salle Men's Chorus, 2 years

Past music experience

-- Organist for 11 years

-- School organist in grammar school

-- Church organist for 5 years

-- Plans for the future are to graduate from high school and major in medicine, perform in Musical Theater.

***

1980

I am Jim Malan and I am auditioning for the part of valedictorian of the De La Salle graduation class of 1980. My reason for trying out for this position is simple:

I feel that I can take the general ideas and attitudes of how the class as a whole sees themselves and convey them in such a manner that teachers, families, friends, relations and students can best understand them.

As to my involvement in school activities over the past four years: I participated on the Spartan swim team and a school newspaper my freshman year. I was a member of the Liturgical planning committee my second year and a member of the Rally Club for two years. I served as Sophomore Class President and held the student body office of Representative at large my junior year. I was a member of the De La Salle/Carondelet mixed chorus the past three years, as well as entertaining in the 1978 Variety Show and the show tomorrow night. I have been an active member in "Company," working on stage and backstage in various dramas and comedies, performing supporting and leading roles in the past four musicals. I participated in a production in the De La Salle Summer School. I've received various awards at the past three academic award nights and won the BankAmerica award in drama this past month. I have been on the honor roll for my duration at De La Salle and presently hold a 3.6 grade point average.

As stated earlier, I am trying for this position because I feel that I can represent the class. De La Salle has given me so much during my years here and you could say that I feel obligated to give it something in return. Being class valedictorian would be the best way that I know—to express my deep appreciation and love for the school.

De La Salle opened its door to its tenth freshman class—and 170 some boys, most strangers, appeared in the halls, ready to start their high school education, ready for the classes, the sports, the rallies— ready for the friendships that would soon determine the class community.

De La Salle has definitely supplied our class with beneficial opinions, attitudes and experiences. Likewise, our class has given De La Salle much the same in return. As the saying goes, "You get out of something what you put into it." Well it goes without saying that the men that you see before you have put much of their time, spirit, knowledge and companionship into this school. In return we have received a well rounded education encompassing academics, spiritual, psychological and physical development. We have held in our hands strength, compassion, friendship, success—many of the experiences that attribute turning a boy into a man.

From becoming the Freshman Football Catholic Athletic League champs to the much enjoyed Sophomore Class Picnic, to the overwhelming win of Fall Festival ticket sales, to the Junior Christmas Party, Junior and Senior Proms, retreats and Senior Breakfast, we have faithfully exhibited this strength, compassion and success.

This graduation ceremony is only the physical culmination of the four years of excellence. I'm sure that the spirit of this class will remain at De La Salle for many years to come.

We leave De La Salle to continue onto the next stop of our lives. But all leave with the great spirit and self-confidence that one acquires from participation in such a school as this. Some of us will take this spirit to colleges and universities—others will take it to jobs or careers that await them. But whatever our future quest may be, we know that in ourselves, we carry the tradition and excellence of De La Salle.

***

Jim Malan, 1980

Fantasy/Mystery

I totally agree with the article on Fantasy that I read yesterday. I believe that any form of fantasy need for a person to live a "normal and satisfied" life. I say "normal and satisfied," not in the sense that everyone's life is "normal," but rather to mean that the act of fantasy is, shall we say a healthy necessity. I realize of course, that too much fantasy can be detrimental to any one person. But then again I'd hate to see what our lives would be like today without the help of those "crazy fanatics" who dreamed the impossible. As technology progresses, so does man's ability to fantasize where once it was considered "irrational" to think about flying across continents, now it is "irrational" to thing about flying to a star. And when, if ever, we reach a star, it will be considered "irrational" to do something else.

Men will always fantasize, no matter how much they have. Why??

Because from a fantasy comes thoughts. These thoughts are conveyed and picked up. Then they are put to use, built upon, and improved. Then they are constructed—and before too long—this once fantasy of the mind has become the reality of the present.

***

Jim Malan, 1980

Theology and Lit.

I can't even begin to describe the feeling that came over me on that spring morning. I stood out on the front lawn, opened the letter and began reading it.

"The government of the United States greets you."

I suddenly felt sick. It was as if my whole stomach contracted into nothing. I couldn't believe that I had actually been drafted.

I cried for weeks. I was so solemn and too depressed to do anything. My school grades fell like rocks. It wasn't so much that I didn't want to go to war, as it was the fact of giving up four years of my life. I had so many plans.

To go to college, then enter Med School, and become a doctor. Now, it all seemed to vanish.

My parents were very upset. I can remember my mother spending hours trying to think up excuses why I wouldn't have to fight. It was no use, my physical checked out and I was given my boot camp assignment.

I tried to enter camp with an open mind. I was over the depression by the fact that my "future" would have to be postponed, so I decided that I'd make the best of it. I adopted a philosophy "If thousands of other guys my age can go through it, then so can I."

I don't think that I was afraid of being hurt or getting killed. Naturally I thought about this many times, but many people had assured me that I would not see any battle since the fighting had not really begun, at least for the United States.

Well, boot camp was worse than I had ever dreamed. I can sum up those nine agonizing weeks in one word "dehumanizing." I couldn't believe what I was seeing. The way we were treated was awful. Up every morning at six marching miles every day. Called by a number—or a name mispronounced, made fun of last name, if we were lucky. I was so homesick and so upset, but I didn't dare let it show for fear of being ridiculed. I just stuck it out as best I could.

I'll never forget how I first felt when a rifle was placed in my hands. It was so heavy and so cold. I didn't want to shoot it. I didn't want to pull that trigger, but I had to. We had target practice for hours each day. Then we ran. We ran miles in heavy green uniforms with helmets, in the middle of summer heat. Then more target practice. I can still hear the endless hours of ear shattering gunshot. I swore then and there I would never own a gun.

Of the nine weeks of drills, running, headaches, gunshot, and just plain depression, the worst part was hand-to-hand combat. I could handle taking shots at real live people; even if we were using blanks. I couldn't handle shoving that bayonet into a dummy. It didn't make sense. Why were we doing this, to serve what purpose? After the nine weeks, we had a couple days leave before our next assignment. One night, all the guys got pretty drunk. We came back to the barracks and everyone was all hyper and screaming and jumping around. One of the guys picked up a bayonet and kiddingly challenged another to a fake sword fight. They started around the room, clashing bayonets and yelling "on guard." This little scene amused everyone including myself. One of these men hit the other's "sword" very hard. The bayonet went flying through the air and hit me right at my ankle. Before I knew what had happened there was an onrush of blood—my blood.

It was then that I panicked. I screamed and thrashed around. The others were shocked that such an accident could've happened. I passed out from blood loss. The next time I woke up I was in a hospital bed at the base hospital. I had surgery and now had a cast on my lower leg. I learned that I would have to stay in bed for eight to ten weeks. This pleased me to no end. For a while at least I was contented to know that I wouldn't have to go to war.

The following eight weeks were almost entirely spent in deep thought. I knew that I had changed. I could feel it. I felt differently than I had felt before I received that letter. I viewed myself differently, I was somewhat proud of myself, proud of the fact that I went through what I had dreaded the most, and endured it.

After eight weeks, it was found out that the bones in my ankle were not healing properly. I went back into surgery and had metal pins and discs inserted. I was bedridden for six more weeks. The topper was that I was assured that I didn't have to re-enter the military because of the operation.

My relief and happiness was overwhelming. I was never so happy in all my life. I was so glad it was over. I could go back to school and carry out my plans.

Of course there was something that bothered me. Something different about me. I wasn't the same boy with the dreams. I looked at my life differently. Yes—I did have the same goals and same thoughts; but in a different way. It's so hard to explain. I just felt "different." In a slight sense, I was glad that I had gone through that "dehumanizing" experience." It had made me think of how I treat others. It gave me more drive to do what I want to. It convinced me to really make something out of myself. Why? I'm not positively sure. But I do know one thing. Every time I feel like putting someone down or not doing my work, I just glance down at the scar just above my left ankle.

Believe me, as much as I hated being drafted I thank my lucky stars for that scar.

***

Daily Log

James Malan 2/7/80

Right now my daily activities are pretty much wrapped up in the musical. These past couple days have shown a lot of progress in the show. I am slowly coming out of my depression that the show would never come off. My only hope now is that the orchestra will be good. I have this awful feeling however that once again the orchestra is going to blow it for us.

I'm also worried about the "Sit down, you're rockin' the boat" and I just hope to God that I get a mic this year that works.

I was really depressed about my classes on Monday, but I am slowly coming out of that too.

My first one "Life Styles" looks like it's going to turn out ok. This one is going to be good and I hope I do good in Physics.

It looks like "Senioritis" is really settling in. I have no want to do any work, and I better stop writing now because I'm 22 pages behind in the book for class. Just like me.

***

Dialogue w/Persons

2/8/80

T _ _ _ -- I've only known T _ _ _ for about eight weeks. Since we went to the Xmas dance, we have gone out almost every week. It seems like we like each other and enjoy each other's company very much. I chose her to write about because this time she is who I mostly think about, because I want this relationship to develop further. I feel funny though because I know how I feel about her, but I'm not sure how she feels about me. People tell me how she feels and sometimes I see this in her.

But I'm not really sure.

I get the feeling she likes me too.

***

Dialogue with Events/Situations

Jim Malan 2/21/80

I don't think I like this situation that I'm in with T _ _ _ It's not that I don't like her. That's not it at all. It's that we kinda live two different lives. One—at school with everybody, and the other, with ourselves. She is so different with me.

Maybe she doesn't want people to know you two are going out—No, I don't think that's it. Whenever we are alone she's so nice and quite funny. I have a great time with her and I'm pretty sure she has a great time with me too.

Then what's the problem? I'm not sure. I guess it's just her attitude. She knows that I really like her. At times, from the way she talks, I get the feeling that she likes me too. But I never really see anything to prove this statement true.

Do you think that you are trying to be too possessive? I don't know. I don't want to be. I want her to have a good time and out with her friends. But I know that she wants to go out with me.

She kids around a lot with me, sometimes I don't know when to take her seriously. She is so popular and so beautiful, smart, funny, sensitive . . . she's great. I really like her family and I know they like me too!!

So what is really the problem?

I wish I knew. I hate to come right out and say that I think that she's really great, because of the way she might take it. I don't want some long relationship to come out of this. But I don't want it to be casual either. I just wish I knew how she really felt.

The only way you can do this is to talk to her about it.

I know she's so—I don't know—different from other girls. I feel so good when I go out with her. We go out a lot and we talk on the phone for hours every day. When we are alone everything is great. But at school I feel weird around her. This isn't her family. We both have our separate set of friends, that we like a lot. We spend a lot of time with them. I just hope that things only get better. I really do want to keep going out with her—I think she's fantastic!

***

Jim Malan

2/22/80

<u>Dialogue with Body</u>

Look Jim, you know that this body is weary. Do you know what you've been putting me through, the past couple weeks? This musical is driving me crazy.

Sorry! But wait till you go through the coming weeks. I sure hope that you can "stomach it." Ha! Ha!

Just try to give me a little rest.

I see that I'm going to have to get you in shape.

Fine, but for now, let's just take it easy, so I can recuperate.

***

Jim Malan

Daily Log

2/26/80

Today I am extremely tired to the point when I can barely keep my eyes open. Of course, it's because of Tech. week.

I really need my rest but there is no time. I'm slowly falling behind in a couple of my classes.

On the bright side, the show does seem to be coming along good, and I am excited about it. I just hope that we have full houses for each performance. (I also hope that I get a good part in West Side Story.)

***

Jim Malan

Daily Log

Feb. 29, 1980

OPENING NITE!! For Guys and Dolls

I'm really excited, especially after the show we put on for the student matinee. It was great!! The show really went off well. I'm now past the point of tired, but God am I excited. The house is almost sold out and my family and friends are coming. I know it will be good. Opening nights are always good. There's a certain electricity that flows through each cast member and this makes us put on a great show. I wish these ten hours would pass faster . . .

***

Jim Malan, March 4, 1980

Dialogue w/ events

<u>Event – opening night!!</u>

Opening night was fantastic. We got a great big standing ovation. The audience laughed at every joke. They were with us the whole way.

It was great. But didn't you expect that kind of reaction??

Yea, but not to the extent that we got. The audience was on their feet even before the curtain call began.

Did you yourself put on a good performance?

I think I did just fine. Please don't think I am bragging but after my last number "Sit down, you're rockin' the boat," Joe had to say his line three times because the audience seemed to applaud forever and no one heard his line at all.

Did that make you feel good or not??

Are you going to be able to keep on doing good shows for the rest of the run??

I hope so. Tomorrow's going to be hard though. The second night is not as good as opening night.

But I think it will be good. I also think that this is the year that we will all get straight standing ovations every night.

**

Daily Log

3-6-80

Today I am depressed. The student matinee went lousy. The audience wasn't receptive at all. They were dead. Also, the cast as a whole kind of botched it up. Overall it was a low standard show.

But that's not all—

I am falling so far behind in my classes that it isn't funny. I am pages behind in Theology and Lit, and even farther behind in Physics. I really have to start catching up but I am constantly tired and I'm missing too much school because of the student matinees.

On the bright side I am happy because today I got accepted to UCLA—I'm not really "happy"—just relieved. I feel this way because right now I am totally fed up with school and I don't want to think about college. But deep down—I'm happy.

***

Jim Malan 3/11/80

The memory that is most clear right now is when my sister and grandparents and I went to the Montreal Summer Olympic Games in 1976.

My sister and I were in New Jersey visiting my grandparents. In July, we decided to drive up to Maine to visit my uncle. From there, we decided to go to Montreal.

My favorite Olympic sport to watch is men's and women's gymnastics. I was so happy when we got tickets. I remember seeing Nadia and Olga wrapping their rubber bodies around those poles and jumping like they had springs on their feet.

Another highlight was seeing Bruce Jenner win the Decathlon. Also watching John Naber win a couple of gold medals.

The best part was flying home on the plane with 3 Olympic swimmers who had 1 gold, silver and bronze. I actually got to see and touch a gold medal. That was fantastic.

***

Jim Malan

Theology & Lit 3/15/80

If a picture paints a thousand words,

Then why can't I paint you?

The words will never show,

The "you" I've come to know.

If a face could launch a thousand ships, then where am I to go?

There's no one home but you

You're all that's left me to.

And when my love for life is running dry

You come and pour yourself on me

If a man could be two places at one time—

I'd be with you

Tomorrow and today

Beside you all the way.

Then one by one the stars will all come out.

Then you and I will <u>simply</u>

<u>Fly away</u>

***

3/20/80

"Intersections"

The past couple of days have been very confusing for me. I've just come to realize something about my future.

Since freshman year my goal in life has been to become a doctor. I've always had an interest in medicine, my mother's a nurse, I do well in science and I love to visit hospitals. My parents really want me to be a doctor—and they are thrilled to see me pursuing such a wonderful career.

I've also had a great interest in drama and music. I have never ever considered this career for one reason and one reason only—the outlook on making a decent living. I know that if a doctor and an actor got the same pay and/or the chances of success in drama were as good as in medicine, that I would pursue the drama career.

I've decided that I am going ahead with the career in medicine. If I absolutely hate it, then I will see what happens.

I just hope that this is a good decision.

***

Jim Malan

Theology & Lit

3/22/80

Dialogue w/ Events

Well, I really didn't want to go up to Reno with Patti, but I'm sure glad that I did now.

Yea, you really looked like you were having a great time.

It was great staying with two guys who were in the MGM show.

I know you didn't expect that. You should have seen your face during the MGM show.

I know, God, that was the most spectacular show that I've ever seen. I couldn't believe my eyes. And the best part was actually knowing five people in the show and then eating dinner with them afterwards.

You certainly needed that little vacation.

Don't I know it! It was a great trip.

***

Lousy Day

Jim Malan March 25, 1980

Today was a lousy day. My parents left for Reno. I was up all night trying to catch up on my Physics because all the labs are due today. At midnight I wasn't finished, so I decided that I had to skip blocks 1-4 (sorry Mr. O) so that I could catch up. At 6:45 that morning my sister Diane called up K _ _ _ , whom I said that I'd drive to school. I told her that they would have to find another ride. K _ _ _ said that she wouldn't drive and that my sister should get me out of bed to drive them anyway. Diane called M _ _ _, who couldn't drive either. Well, I wasn't about to drive all the way out to school and then back to my Physics. Diane called K _ _ _ back to ask how they were going to get to school. K _ _ _ got extremely mad and said "that I better get my butt out of bed and pick her up." Diane told her that I couldn't drive them to school. At this point, K _ _ _ somehow "miraculously" got hold of a car and was able to pick Diane up. When she arrived, she slammed open the front door screaming her head off and calling me everything in the book. She said that I was doing this deliberately that her parents were going to tell my parents and that I was In so much F _ _ _ trouble. I told her to get the hell out of my house. What really burns me up is that whenever she wants to stop somewhere on the way home from school, or me to wait after school for her, or when she wants a ride somewhere, I do it without thinking twice. Now when I imposed something on her she acts like a child.

***

Theology and Literature

Jim Malan 3/27/80

Dialogue with Society

All right now—you guys have no right getting mad at me. None of this was my fault.

But if you didn't drive her to school.

I told her an hour before that I wouldn't go to school and she still wanted me to get up and drive her anyway.

She had plenty of time to find a ride.

But she was really mad.

Mad?? I'm really pissed. No one is going to barge into my house and start yelling at me like she did.

Nobody!!

She is not getting another ride from me anywhere until she apologizes.

She's going to be real stubborn. For once, I'm not going to give in. I am going to be just as stubborn.

***

Jim Malan

Daily Log

3-27-80

This morning has been great. I saw Dr. Clarence and he gave me the videotape of Guys and Dolls. I've been waiting for this for a long time. I can't wait to get home and see what we all look like on television.

Also, I'm feeling really good because I just found out that I won a Bank of America certificate. My problem is that I don't know in what category. My first thought is in Drama but I'm really not sure. Anyway—so far my day is going great.

***

Jim Malan

Theology and Lit

Final Paper

Probably the most important thing that I have gotten out of this class is that every single person had his or her own uniqueness. Granted, I did know this fact before, but it became that much clearer in the way that we took each story and contrasted it to the others. This "contrasting" took qualities of one character in one novel and made me notice both differences as well as similarities to the other characters in the other novels. Using these characteristics, one could actually predict how one of the characters would answer when asked a certain question; or would react when face with a certain situation.

The question that I wish to tackle in this paper is a very abstract one. "What makes up a human being?"

I wish to answer this in the emotional sense. I know that there are "umpteen" factors that go into the creating of a single human being. But I've also seen throughout our readings that a person possesses one or two "outstanding" qualities which are displayed throughout his or her daily life. I would like to take each quality and expand on that, in order to find out, however roughly, what actually does make up this special human being.

I thought that Barrabas was perhaps the most depressing book that I have read in a great while. There was little happiness at all seen in the book, with Barrabas as well as with any one other character.

I think that one outstanding quality that Barrabas showed was a kind of "questioning." I don't want to say "curiousness" because I don't believe that he was curious in the way that we think of it. So I'd like to leave his characteristic as "questioning."

What did he question? Well, the obvious is—"Is there a God?" He was very confused and frankly, there was no reason not to be. So many people told him so many "unbelievable things."

Was he released so that God could be crucified? If so, why him?

What a burden—to know that you, a convicted criminal, were released so that an innocent 'savior" could be murdered.

Did his "new life" have to have some meaning? Why was he given this new start? Was there something that he should do to repay somebody? If so, what and who?

I think that his life was filled with signs: the retarded, girl, the fat lady, his so-called friends, the man in prison, the inscribed disc around his neck. Almost every situation he found himself in could have some meaning, some "answer" to his questions. But how could he know which answer, if any, were correct?

Should he believe that this ill-clad, underfed man named Jesus was actually God the Savior? No wonder it was hard for him to believe. There were so many questions and few, few answers.

And so it is today. People's lives are centered around question after question. It is very hard to find answers. Answers about faith, death, afterlife, and God. No one is there to give the answers. They must be decided by each person. If they believe, then their question is answered. If they need an answer—they search.

Night ranked right up there with Barrabas as far as depression goes. The only difference was that every so often, there would be a "bright spot" in the novel in which there would be some hope among the people.

The person with the most "hope" was Elizar. Every word that he spoke was somehow derived from the hope that he had in the back of his mind. Hope that the war would soon be over. Hope that they would be liberated. Hope that he could get an extra morsel of bread for his father and himself. Hope that his sister and his mother weren't dead. Hope that this nightmare would soon be over.

I think that people in this day and age have practically no hope when compared with Elizar. Sure, one might hope for a new car, or hope that he lives to be ninety. But when a human being, and a young boy at that, selfishly thinks up many ways to get a portion of bread or a teaspoon of soup; that is true hope.

I know that that kind of hope isn't seen today. People may wish something was, but there is no back to it, no sincerity. At least not when compared to Elizar's. We give up too easily. If our hopes of one thing don't materialize, we start to hope that something else will happen. If the majority of the people today were faced with a similar situation to that of Elizar's, I'm very sure that there would be a lot of hope lost.

In All Quiet on the Western Front, it is true that both Paul, as well as the other men (boys) had both questions and hope. When would their "hell" be over? "I hope that it is over soon."

But the main aspect that Paul encountered was that of "change." This became evident when he went home on leave. His whole attitude was changed. It was very difficult for him to come home. He had been through so much in the war that no one that wasn't on the front right beside him would believe. He changed his way of thinking. He changed his goals. He changed his whole outlook on life. I didn't really see this until he wrote the letter to his mother saying that he was going back to the front—"his home." That struck me as his real change. For anyone to say that his once loved and cherished family and the house that he lived in for all his life was not home, indicates a change, a drastic one.

This was Paul's changing point. He was now a man. He had different questions, different hopes. They had all changed from what they had been. The question that remains in my mind is; did he change for the better or for the worse? (Ask this question to your students next year. It'll make them think.)

In The Heart is the Lonely Hunter, Mick's life is filled with everything I have thus far talked about. She questions, she hopes, and she changes. But I think that her most outstanding characteristic is her ability to "wish." Her life is filled with wishing. She wishes she was grown up. She wishes people would understand. She wishes she could write music. She wishes to be like Mozart. She wishes to be befriended to Mr. Singer. At times, she wishes she was dead. I don't think that she makes these wishes selfishly. They are all simple wishes that I believe she is entitled to. She has the right to wish. After all, she has so many things to offer if only the right opportunities would arise. So why not wish for the opportunity. I would have loved to see her develop into a beautiful lady, win a musical scholarship to college, become a world-renowned doctor, and find a cure for Mr. Singer. And I'm sure that if that were within the realm of her imagination, that she would wish for it too.

Her wishes, however trivial, were at least sincere. They were for things that she would enjoy and develop and be good at. They weren't "greedy" wishes but rather "needy" ones. And you know that if I was her fairy godmother, all her wishes would come true.

In The Little Prince, it was obvious that the prince was somewhat irritated at his elders. He claimed that they didn't understand him or anything that he thought. Although he didn't say it in so many words, he believed that as one grew older, on "decayed" in the mind. They got so wrapped up in their confused, mixed up lives, that they forgot what it was once like to be vulnerable and unknowledgeable. But one can be unknowledgeable and still understand. The Little Prince understood many things at his own intellectual level. The problem that he had was "lowering" his thoughts to the level of adults in order to communicate with them. I say "lower" rather than "raise" because even though adults' intellectual capacities are somewhat higher than children's, they are so bogged down with figures and calculations and worries that children haven't even begun to think about, that they can't understand the oversimplified yet very expressive thinking patterns of young 'ns.

Although this book could primarily be considered a children's book, it contains more "hidden meanings" that many adults couldn't understand. It's oversimplified intellectually. People have to lower themselves and by lowering I mean to forget about cares and woes and whether the PG&E bill is going to be too high and whether they should've ordered power windows on their car and whether the plane gets in at 9:52 or 9:55. Forget about their trivial aspects of life and chances are that you'll see the simple joy giving aspects of life that you knew as a little boy or girl.

And so you have it—The Characteristics that make up a human being are questions, hope, change, wishing, and understanding. Right??? Not by a long shot. It's impossible to say "this is what makes up a human being and anything else is an alien."

But there are some aspects that a human possesses. After all, a person that doesn't question—knows all. A person that doesn't hope—has everything. A person that doesn't change—is immortal. A person that doesn't wish—is satisfied. And a person that doesn't misunderstand—understands everything.

And there is only one person that knows, has everything, is immortal, is satisfied, and understands . . .

(Teacher's note: Powerful ending!)

***

Danville Youth killed when auto hits tree

James J. Malan, an 18-year-old resident of Danville, was killed early Sunday morning when he apparently fell asleep at the wheel of his car and the vehicle struck a tree on Morninghome Road (two blocks from his home).

Malan had been performing as a dancer for the annual Miss Walnut Creek Pageant and had apparently attended a party Saturday night after the pageant before driving himself home, according to Kathy Tomas, executive director of the Walnut Creek Pageant.

***

James Malan

James (Jim) J. Malan, in Walnut Creek, on August 24, 1980. A resident of Danville. Loving son of Mr. & Mrs. John Malan; brother of Diane & Linda Malan; grandson of Marie & Roxie Georgette of Walnut Creek; nephew of John E. Georgette of Walnut Creek; also survived by many relatives in New Jersey. A native of Pennsylvania and a former resident of Cherry Hill, New Jersey. Age 18 years. Organist at St. Anne's Catholic Church, Rossmoor. Employed by Bank of America in W.C. A 1976 graduate from St.

Isidore's grade school, Danville; a 1980 honor graduate of De La Salle High School in Concord. Enrolled to attend pre-med at U.C.L.A. in September. Member of the Thespian Club. Performed in many plays & musicals in the area for the past 4 years. (At Willows in Concord & Civic Arts in W.C.)

***

James John Malan

Born to us April 27, 1962, Born to God August 24, 1980

Dear God,

Eighteen years ago you sent this world, this community, and in particular, a family, the Malans, a delightful new gift, JIMMY. He is a gift that will remain forever with us. We are deeply grateful. We have learned something else about your "Gift-Giving." You really do love us very much. Jimmy is a proof of your love. He gave himself to us in so many ways, and now he has given himself to you because you need him. It helps us to remember Jesus did this and continues His "Gift-Giving" each day. We are thankful to you God because Jimmy was one of the best examples of Jesus that we know. Until we join Jimmy and Jesus in the Resurrected LIFE, be with us each day. Amen/Alleluia

Fr. Tom Ryan

***

James John Malan

1962-1980

Company dedicates this year's musical to a dear friend and fellow performer.

It takes a special person to be able to touch so many individuals in such a short time, and in such a positive way. Jim Malan was that special person. He clearly shined in each of his many roles. He sparkled as student, brother, entertainer, and friend.

In the theatre, Jim was a true professional. He brought life and movement to a silent character in a black and white script, whether it be Speed, Friend of Valentine, Harry, Doolittle's sidekick, Marryin' Sam, or Nicely Nicely Johnson. I feel honored to have been given the opportunity to work with such a master craftsman.

Good friends and slight acquaintances knew of Jim's caring nature. He responded to his friends beyond the call of duty. He was gentle and kind, quite different than any other man of eighteen, yet the same. Jim Malan was full of hope, and he always searched for the light at the end of the tunnel, that heaven "over the rainbow." Jim—I think you've found it.

Ann Lewis

***

James Malan

As his Willows Theatre friends remember him

The Scarecrow in the Wizard of Oz, summer 1980

Will Parker in Oklahoma! Fall 1980

To a Star

There is a special bond between performers. They compete with the fury of any Olympic athlete yet will begrudge no colleague their chance at fame. Hey are the first to laugh and cry, and the first to come to their feet applauding. There is no difference of color, religious or social background on stage, richman and poorman share equal wealth under the colored lights. They are more than friend or family, they are all part of one dream. When one becomes a star it is a minor triumph for us all, calming our fear of failure and reinforcing our persistent faith that we too may reach the end of our rainbow.

On the morning of the 24th of August, 1980 a fellow performer played his final scene. It was not a long monotonous performance but the quick and tragic exit of a true professional, leaving not a dry eye or untouched heart.

Jim Malan, I applaud you and look not with fear but with patient anticipation to the day when I too will take my final bow on this stage and join you as a new and shining star at the end of the rainbow.

--by Keith Tatman

October 1980

***

"REACH OUT"

Dedicated to Jim Malan

James John Malan — 1962-1980

A vibrant and talented member of our pageant family

Performed with us in the past four pageants

WE "REACH OUT" TO YOU, OUR FRIEND . . . TONIGHT

1980

Willows Theatre hosts 'Oklahoma'

Two Danville men star in the Concord Community Arts production of "Oklahoma!" now running at the Willows Theatre in Concord through Nov. 10. They are (left) Cliff Ballou, who plays the menacing hired hand, Jud, and James Malan, who plays Will Parker, suitor of Ado Annie, the girl who "Cain't Say No." The show runs every Friday and Saturday evening at 8 p.m. as well as Sundays, Oct. 21 and 28, at 2 p.m. and this Sunday and next as well as Nov. 4 at 7 p.m. It will also play Thursdays, Oct. 18 and Nov. 1 and 8, at 8 p.m. Very limited tickets are available; interested persons should call 798-6525 or stop by the Willows Theatre Box Office, 1975 Diamond Boulevard, Concord, open noon to 6 p.m. Tuesday through Friday and noon to 4 p.m. Saturday and Sunday.

JAMES JOHN MALAN
1962 - 1980

Company dedicates this year's musical to
a dear friend and fellow performer

James John Malan
Born to us April 27, 1962 Born to God August 24, 1980

Dear God,
　Eighteen years ago you sent this world, this community, and in particular, a family, the Malans, a delightful new gift, JIMMY. He is a gift that will remain forever with us. We are deeply grateful. We have learned something else about your 'Gift-Giving.' You really do love us very much. Jimmy is a proof of your love. He gave himself to us in so many ways, and now he has given himself to you because you need him. It helps us to remember Jesus did this and continues His 'Gift-Giving' each day. We are thankful to you God because Jimmy was one of the best examples of Jesus that we know. Until we join Jimmy and Jesus in the Resurrected LIFE, be with us each day. Amen/Alleluia
　　　　　　　　　　　　　　　—Fr. Tom Ryan

JAMES JOHN MALAN
1962 - 1980

Company dedicates this year's musical to a dear friend and fellow performer

Li'l Abner

Two Gentlemen of Veron

Guys and Dolls

My Fair Lady

　It takes a special person to be able to touch so many individuals in such a short time, and in such a positive way. Jim Malan was that special person. He clearly shined in each of his many roles. He sparkled as student, brother, entertainer, and friend.
　In the theatre, Jim was a true professional. He brought life and movement to a silent character in a black and white script, whether it be Speed, Friend of Valentine, Harry, Doolittle's sidekick, Marryin Sam, or Nicely-Nicely Johnson; I feel honored to have been given the opportunity to work with such a master craftsman.
　Good friends and slight acquaintances knew of Jim's caring nature. He responded to this friends beyond the call of duty. He was gentle and kind, quite different than any other man of eighteen, yet the same. Jim Malan was full of hope, and he always searched for the light at the end of the tunnel, that heaven "over the rainbow." Jim — I think you've found it.
　　　　　　　　　　　　　　　　　　　Ann Lewis

James Malan

AS HIS
WILLOWS THEATRE
FRIENDS
REMEMBER HIM

THE SCARECROW
in
THE WIZARD OF OZ
summer 1980

WILL PARKER
in
OKLAHOMA!
fall 1980

TO A STAR

There is a special bond between performers. They compete with the fury of any Olympic athlete yet will begrudge no colleague their chance at fame. They are the first to laugh and cry, and the first to come to their feet applauding. There is no difference of color, religious or social background on stage, richman and poorman share equal wealth under the colored lights. They are more than friend or family, they are all part of one dream. When one becomes a star it is a minor triumph for us all, calming our fear of failure and reinforcing our persistent faith that we too may reach the end of our rainbow.

On the morning of the 24th of August, 1980 a fellow performer played his final scene. It was not a long monotonous performance but the quick and tragic exit of a true professional, leaving not a dry eye or untouched heart.

Jim Malan, I applaud you and look not with fear but with patient anticipation to the day when I too will take my final bow on this stage and join you as a new and shining star at the end of the rainbow

— by Keith Tatman

Jim's Musicals and Plays

De La Salle High School

Willows Theater, Concord

1976   Our Town

1977   Two Gentlemen of Verona

1977   Diary of Anne Frank

1978   My Fair Lady

1978   Godspell

1979   Li'l Abner

1979   Oklahoma (Willows)

1980   Guys and Dolls

1980   Wizard of Oz (Willows)

　　　Miss Walnut Creek 1977-1980

　　　(4 years)

　　　Reno Musical 1979

IT'S MY LIFE

The Biography of James Malan

P.T. Barlow

The Cover

Leslie Carrasa's gift to the Malan family at the time of Jim's rebirth to another life

Accompanying her drawing was this expression of her feelings:

>With all my love
>
>And all my heart,
>
>This, is for you
>
>In honor of your new start.
>
>Your caring eyes and fabulous grin
>
>Has captured us all deep within.
>
>You look upon us as we look up to you
>
>And each is born into something new.
>
>With all my love, and all my heart,
>
>Les'

PREFACE

The mementos in this book were not saved with the idea that they would be chronicled. They are presented with respect as insights into the life of the young man who valued them enough to keep them.

Just as pencil marks on a doorjamb can be used to record the physical growth of a youngster, the drawings and written work one saves can characterize the evolutionary maturation of an individual. By compiling these keepsakes and intertwining the remembrances of his family and friends to give continuity and perception is to share, in part at least, the formative years of Jim Malan's life.

Jim was a "people person," outgoing and gregariously vivacious. Appreciating that each friendship was both unique and personal to him, Jim's relationships with people are presented compositely.

The title is a phrase often used by our subject and was selected by his mother.

CHAPTER 1

A new day and Jim awoke to the familiar surroundings of his room. There wasn't much space left of the pale blue walls. They were covered with memorabilia: playbills and programs from the productions he had appeared in, athletic and academic certificates he had earned, dance favors, swimming as well as track and field ribbons. The top of the built-in chest of drawers was covered with framed photographs of family and friends. Articles of clothing, pieces of costumes that he had worn during the run of various plays were tacked here and there. The shelves above his desk held an assortment of medals from swim meets, a trophy for a ballroom dance contest won in elementary school, and souvenirs he had from vacation trips. He liked this room—his room.

Jim reached out and turned off the alarm that had yet to ring. This was the morning he was going to write his valedictory speech. Well, a speech he hoped to give at the commencement exercises, there was a competition being held to determine which of the scholastically qualified seniors would deliver the farewell address. It had not been an easy decision to make. Attempting to represent the nucleus of a school had given him cause for long periods of reflective thought. Actually it was another competitor who had convinced him to tryout. Jim had not told his parents or two sisters of his valedictorian aspiration. His grandparents, NaNa and PopPop (that's what he called them as a very little boy and was by now a heartfelt endearment) didn't know either. As he stretched his six foot two inch frame within the bed he mentally pleasured at the prospect that they would all be so surprised and proud on graduation day if he were to be the valedictorian. Should he win that honor he was going to keep it a secret. He imagined them all sitting in the audience and experiencing his introduction as a speaker. He knew it wouldn't make any difference to those who loved him if he got to give the speech or not. Those who loved him were not only proud of, but very supportive of, his endeavors. Hey! There were hassles, curfews, restrictions and a few encounters he would prefer not to think about. Yet, bottom line, his family measured up to, if not past, those of his friends. He loved them all and was secure with the knowledge that he was loved in return. Growing to eighteen hadn't always been easy—on any of them—but the positive experiences far outweighed the negative. Now he wanted to give a gift to the givers.

Swinging his legs off the side of the bed Jim sat on the edge of the mattress. As he raised his hand to his head his fingers separated the thick mass of sandy-blonde, wavy hair and he looked out the window. It would be another hot day in California. No clouds in the sky. A great day for the beach—except for school—except today he was going to write a speech.

He took a few steps to his desk, seated himself, placed a sheet of paper in the typewriter, paused a moment and typed.

My name is Jim Malan and I am auditioning for the position of Valedictorian of De La Salle's graduating class of 1980.

CHAPTER 2

My reasons for trying out for the position are simple.

Jim read the sentence. Was that thought true? He had lived most of his life in Danville, a town with a population of about 18,000. You didn't know everyone in a town this size but you didn't worry about violent crimes that large city dwellers worried about.

His elementary schooling had been in the small parochial school in town. With only one class per grade at St. Isidore's you pretty much went through the eight grades with the same classmates. In a class of forty even when someone moved and a new kid came in it didn't take very long to get to know them. He had made some very good friends in that school, boys and girls both. They still went around together at times because after graduation most of the girls went to Carondelet High School and the guys to De La Salle High. One very good thing about both of these schools was that they were right across the street from each other. Since neither school was coeducational, their geographic location was important to their student body memberships!

Yeah, thinking back to elementary school days, life was simple then. It may not have seemed like it at the time but it seemed like it now. Leaning back in his chair Jim grinned as he thought about being in grade school. It was in the sixth grade that he entered his writing era. He would write, cast, direct and sometimes act in a play. There would be parts for about half of his classmates and the rest would help with scenery. It had been great fun and one Christmas play was pretty good. He still had a copy of that play. There had been poems also: Spring is Here and Look All Around, he remembered working on each. He had always written letters, perhaps an extension of note writing in class! But he had really outdone himself when he wrote, then president, Nixon. The slightest of frowns came on Jim's face as he wondered why Mr. Nixon hadn't answered that letter. That would have been something, a letter from the White House.

It seemed to Jim that when you were first in school everything you did was looked upon as special, wonderful, noteworthy and put on the refrigerator for all to see. His mom was a saver too. She still had a hand print of his when he was in kindergarten. Maybe that is why he had started to save papers and mementos. Or was it the journal that his English teacher required each student to keep throughout the eighth grade?

Focusing his attention on the last line he had typed Jim knew he was correct. His reasons were simple because he had not only liked the schools he had been in, but appreciated them. Placing his fingers lightly on the typewriter keys he watched his thoughts appear on the page.

CHAPTER 3

I feel that I can take the general ideas and attitudes of how the class, as a whole, sees themselves, and convey then in such a manner that teachers, family, friends, relatives, and students can best understand them.

He smiled confidently at the ease with which he had written the sentence. Within the experience of writing his final paper in Theology and Lit there had been a clarifying definitive probing of his opinions and ideals.

It was important to each graduate that they be recognized as an individual: A thinking, feeling, educated adult capable of making their own judgments and decisions. Each had goals and dreams and wanted the chance to achieve them. It was a time to love life, live it to the fullest and make their mark on the world.

Jim himself had geared his studies toward his interest in medicine. He knew the high marks in biology, chemistry, physiology and advanced mathematic courses had a beneficial effect on the application for admission forms he had completed for college. He had applied to the School of Medicine at Stanford University, University of Southern California, University of California Los Angeles, University of California Berkeley and Boston University. So far he had received positive responses from both Boston University and University of California, Los Angeles. Because of the Bio-Medical program that Boston University offered Jim was interested in attending. Consideration had to be given to the fact that out of state fees would be an additional financial obligation, as well as the distance from home. Talking it over with his parents aided Jim in his decision to attend UCLA. He was happy with the decision, especially because UCLA has a notable Theatre Arts Department and acting was a turn on for him.

In a few weeks high school would be over, the placement tests had been completed, the college entrance exam passed, the interest inventory survey results lay neatly on his desk, so much was now experience and the future was excitement. "Romp, frolic and chew on pretty pup snips" he was going to UCLA! Jim picked up the computerized results of his interest inventory and reread it in part.

. . . "Average scores on these scales range between 43 and 57. Scores below 43 are generally considered low and indicate that you probably share few of the characteristics of that theme. Scores above 57 generally are considered high and suggest that many of the characteristics of that theme probably fit you."

His highest score was "65" on the "E-Theme Scale." The printout explained that "E" stood for "Enterprising." The definition given:

"E-Theme people are frequently in sales work because they are good at leading and convincing people. Enthusiastic, self-confident, and dominant, they think up new ways of doing things, are full of energy, and like adventure. They are impatient with work involving many details, or long periods of intellectual effort or concentration. They prefer social situations where they can lead and direct others . . ."

Taking into consideration that the inventory had stipulated, "The descriptions given below list the characteristics for one theme, however, may not fit exactly any one person," there was that familiar mischievous twinkle in his brown eyes because the majority of the description was right-on. He liked people and was pleased that people liked him. To be with a group of friends was the most fun. Well, with the exception of being with Tracy, but even on their dates they usually joined a group sometime through the evening. He also admitted to being able to lead and convince people. From student government to inducing his friends to join him in cold ocean water on overcast days at the beach, people did seem to be comfortable placing their trust in him. As far as enthusiasm and being full of energy, Jim laughed to himself, that was true. Family and friends alike were overly, the way he saw it, concerned that he took on too much. Realizing their interest was for his well being he still told them all the same thing, "It's my life—I've got to live it."

It was interesting that his highest score was in the "Enterprising Theme" because his folks would certainly be in the same category. His dad was a regional manager with the RCA Corporation, a position which required both self-motivation and a lot of traveling. The days when they used to work together on a project had been the best. There had been a lot of projects when they had first moved into this house. He remembered the Saturday they had built the loft in the garage, all day together, hard work, but a fantastic day. And they had designed and installed the sprinkler system, it didn't seem possible that had been five years ago.

Mom sure did fit into the "Enterprising" group. A registered nurse who worked at the nearby hospital and she recently decided to go into real estate sales. The course work and studying for her realtors license while continuing to work at the hospital had been a demanding schedule for her to maintain. But she had done it and he sure was proud of her. No wonder they kept cautioning him to slow down, they knew the physical drain that could come if you didn't use your time and energy wisely.

Glancing at the clock made Jim aware that he had better get back to speech writing. The house was still and he knew that he would have a few hours before the family awakened, but he had better get to it.

CHAPTER 4

Background of my activities: I participated on the Spartan swim team and a school newspaper in my freshman year.

The summer that Jim graduated from grade school he anxiously anticipated getting started at De La Salle High School. He could remember wanting to get involved—really involved in many activities that hadn't been offered to him before. He simply felt wasted when he wasn't doing something. That feeling certainly had not changed in four years! Involved in school, after school—busy, busy, activity was his energy, his happiness—there was so much he wanted to do, had to do, and there seemed to be too little time.

To satisfy a dream he had had for several years, he tried out for the school production of "Our Town" and was cast as "Wally Webb." Jim remembered well the try-outs, rehearsals and the three evenings in early November when the performances were given to the public. That's when his mom first started giving that "double wave" of hers! She'd, almost, stand and wave with both hands. He said it embarrassed him, but he not only looked for it, but counted on it. It was through this play participation that he made most of his friends. The girls from Carondelet and boys from De La Salle combined efforts in theatrical endeavors and the friendships had become deep and long lasting.

Having been on a local swim team for the past five years prior to high school, it was a natural extension of his interest to join the school's team. The fall of 1976 he also joined the local AAU swim team.

Shaking his head from side to side slowly, Jim remembered his schedule. For the first three months of his freshman year he woke at 4:00 am to complete his paper route and get to school for the 5:30 am swim practice which ended at 7:30 am. School classes until 2:30 pm, play rehearsal from 3:00 pm to 5:00 pm. A fast carpool ride to the AAU swim practice from 6:00 pm to 8:00 pm. Dinner by 8:30 pm, homework and in bed by 10:30 pm. After three months of that schedule he knew something would have to go. It was the outside swimming he had relinquished.

Jim's gaze slipped over the program of "Two Gentlemen of Verona" which was on the wall. What a spring he had in his freshman year. He had played the role of "Speed," servant and friend of Valentine (a Gentleman of Verona). He'd been pleased to get the part and had worked hard to give it the best in him. This group was becoming his extended family, faculty advisors and students alike, it was a happy productive time. His family was pleased and proud of his talents. Jim remembered his sisters, Diane and Linda, were still in grade school but they would help him with chores at home so he could keep up with all his activities.

On the weekends he continued to play the organ at church as well as sing in the Folk Group. He had been playing the organ since he was six and had taught himself guitar so he could be in the Folk Group.

Jim hadn't expected to do all this reminiscing. Brother! If this is what you did every time you graduated it was a good thing it didn't happen too often. No sooner had he thought it than he caught sight of the awards above his desk. At the academic awards night, the end of his freshman year he had received three: English, Social Studies and Spanish. His folks had almost popped their buttons. He'd been elected Sophomore Class President that spring and he had kept his promise to himself, he was involved!

Yes, that had been a good year but more was to come. And more had better come on this speech! Jim straightened himself in the chair and reached toward the typewriter's keyboard.

CHAPTER 5

> *I was a member of the Spartan Rally Club for two years, the Liturgy Planning Committee in my second year. I served as Sophomore Class President and a Representative-at-large in the Student Council in my third year. I was a member of the De La Salle-Carondelet High School Mixed Chorus for the past three years as well as entertaining in the 1978 and the Variety Show tomorrow night.*

He had typed the sentences, yet Jim's mind continued to indulge in the memories of the summer of 1976. That had been the first summer he had been involved in the Miss Walnut Creek Pageant. As an entertainer in the festival he had sung and danced with a group of young people, some of the kids from school theatre group were in it. The audience was larger and so was his desire to spend more time on stage.

He had gone back to the AAU Swim Team, just for the summer, but it would keep him in shape for the Spartan Team. The time needed for his paper route had been reduced because he had gotten a Moped. What a feeling that was—zipping along—effortlessly. He relished the thought of the breeze on his face.

There had been the usual outings with his friends, anyone of their parents would take them to a movie or out to the mall and pick them up later. They went to each other's houses and just bummed around or called somebody on the phone. Jim laughed aloud as he thought about the phone; he sure had spent hours and hours on the phone in the past four years.

Was that the summer he had visited NaNa and PopPop or was it the summer before? It was the year his folks had gotten the new station wagon and they had driven cross-country and visited with his grandparents. He enjoyed the close relationship he had with his mother's parents. When he was with them they would ask their friends in and he would play the organ and they would have a sing-fest. There was always an adventure to come. They had a grand tour of New York City. He laughed as he remembered that PopPop had left NaNa and he off at the United Nations building and taken a cab without realizing that his wife had all the money. He had written his folks about that and asked that they save the letter, wonder if that was still around? There had been trips to Maine and Washington D.C. Now he remembered: the trip to New Jersey with his family had been the summer of 1975, because in July of 1976 it was just Diane and he that his grandparents had taken to the Summer Olympic Games in Montreal. They had seen Nadia Comaneci's performance in the women's gymnastics event. Bruce Jenner had won the Decathlon and they had been there to see him. The real highlight of that trip was flying home on the plane with three Olympic swimmers who had won gold, silver and bronze Olympic medals. Jim savored the thought of touching the gold medal. Fantastic!

Back to work man! Let's get with it here—let's see, yeah, September 1976—Sophomore Class President, and the assistant director for the schools production of "The Diary of Anne Frank." That was presented the last part of October. Jim had a flurry of thoughts that included Student Council meetings and the Rally Club. Jim believed in, and gave his all to, each activity he participated in, but the Rally Club promoted the activities of the entire school and that appealed to him.

His second year at De La Salle had culminated with an award in English and a prized membership in the International Thespian Society.

Jim shifted his frame in the chair and made a mental note that he should get some academics in this speech somewhere—of course he could always recite the poem he had written:

>Homework
>
>The teacher tried everything under the sun,
>
>That he hoped would make me get my homework done,
>
>But try as he may,
>
>He'd never succeed,

> Because of the book,
>
> That I'd never read.
>
> He'd try apples and candies and teddy bears, too,
>
> Sports cars and tractors, a brand new kazoo,
>
> Jackets and sweaters and pure woolen socks,
>
> Ice cream and cookies and bagels with lox,
>
> Flowers and post cards and monkeys and cats,
>
> Hoses and hamsters, yes, even gray rats.
>
> And even today, that stupid old teacher,
>
> Wants to give up and become an old preacher,
>
> If only he knew that back in that day,
>
> All that I wanted was one stupid "A."

It sure would get the attention of the faculty and parents! His classmates would howl! Nah, they had all worked too hard for this graduation day. There had been an abundance of lighthearted occasions equaled by studies and the painful experiences of working at personal relationships. The class of '80 had reached yet another goal, together, and it was an important plateau for each of them. It was the last time they would be together as a unit, a class, and regardless of how each man tried to disguise the fact, they were aware that their life would never be quite the same again.

CHAPTER 6

> *I have participated in, and worked backstage in various dramas and comedies and have held a lead in the past four musicals.*

In the spring of '78 he had the role of Harry in "My Fair Lady" it was a pleasure to recall. There seemed to be a special chemistry to that cast, a sparkle that was evident to the audience as much as the performers themselves.

Thinking about it, Jim wondered if it wasn't that he was more sure of himself than he had been before. He had his own transportation by the time of that play and it was easier to make rehearsals than it had been before.

Jim stood up and walked to the window. He looked down from his second floor vantage point at the pool in the back yard. There wasn't a ripple on the water. The sun was inching its way up into the sky.

It was just about the clear the roof of their neighbor's house. How many laps had he swum in how many pools? Hundreds upon hundreds of grueling laps. Early on foggy winter mornings when you were so cold you were blue getting out of the water. Days in the hot sun that burnt your skin and bleached your hair. Still he didn't regret it. Being a swimmer had taught him the necessity of self-discipline, the dedication to hard work needed to succeed, to keep disappointment in proportion and most of all, the need for personal commitment.

He put all of those laps to good use by opening his own swimming school, right down there in their yard. He'd done well too. Little kids who wouldn't swim for other instructors really worked for him. Jim had a special rapport with children. He truly loved them and they seemed to know it. Even after the plays, little kids would come up and ask him for his autograph. He smiled as he turned from the window. Anyway, between giving swimming lessons, getting the organist job at St. Anne's Church and his paper route, he scraped up enough money to buy his first car in June of 1977. A 1968 red Pontiac convertible. All that summer his friends would pile in the car and they would drive around with the top down. As he returned to the desk and sat down he remembered the day they had driven through the newest housing development in their area. They had just been driving along looking at the houses and he saw one with the garage door open. He turned the Pontiac into the drive and pulled into the garage, tooting the horn and called out, "We're here, are you ready to go?" The girls in the car squealed and shrieked and there was pandemonium as his passengers all tried to hide at once. Jim laughed at the thought. Where could anyone hide in a convertible with the top down?

That summer he had made his second Miss Walnut Creek Pageant, again as a dancer in the entertainment segment of the program. In July he participated in the high school summer drama workshop production of "Day by Day" he performed in the scenes from "Godspell."

As he sat down at the desk he looked at the sheet in the machine . . .have held the lead in the past four musicals. "Li'l Abner" was the undertaking of the Carondelet and De La Salle "Company" in his junior year. He had played Marryin' Sam as well as understudying the part of Li'l Abner. It was not unusual for any of the company members to carry one of the leads and also understudy another part—but it did make life interesting. By now, company members had appeared in two or three musicals together and it seemed that each new presentation took on its own personality. Jim was well aware that this was in large part due to the ability of the Drama Department faculty members that worked with them. Those teachers knew their craft and the young people that they worked with. They knew how to draw the best that you had to give and you gave your best, both for the good of the show and to meet your own standards. The company was getting good advanced publicity in the local newspapers and noteworthy reviews. His mom had started a scrapbook, well thought Jim, moms are like that.

It was neat that not only his family, but most of the neighborhood, came to his performances now. Jim knew that he was a part of a whole when he performed. Any cast member was only as good as the support given and received, in his opinion, not just on stage when the audience was looking, but rehearsals, in the wings, it had to be a total commitment.

He thought about his grandparents having moved out to the area during his junior year. They lived just a few miles away and they came to see him too. Jim was aware of the comments made about his "up" personality. He shrugged his shoulders as he wondered how he could be anything else with all the loving support he received. Life was good, his life was good; he wanted to share the feeling.

It was also during his junior year that he had appeared in Walnut Creek Civic Arts Repertory production of "Peter Pan." Walnut Creek was a city about six or seven miles from the town he lived in. Since he had already indulged himself to question how many laps he had swum, Jim wondered how many miles he had traveled back and forth? Closing his eyes he began his calculations. Let's see, Walnut Creek is about six miles from here, the school is seventeen miles, he knew that for sure since he had started paying for his own gas. Oh, it was astronomical! He still had his job as organist on the weekends and worked at the Walnut Creek branch of The Bank of America after school each day—finish the speech and leave the mathematical puzzles for the Rube Cube fans.

November of this senior year he had been Will Parker in the Willows production of Oklahoma. The Willows Theatre was part of the Community Theatre Programs in the City of Concord.

Nicely-Nicely Johnson in "Guys and Dolls" had been the character he portrayed in his last appearance with The Company of De La Salle and Carondelet High Schools. Their March performances somehow seemed a long time ago. There had been much hugging and reliving of their experiences during the past four years. As much as Jim would miss the group, and he knew he would, he still had the part of the Scarecrow in the "Wizard of Oz" at The Willows Theatre coming up and was looking forward to being an entertainer at the Miss Nevada Contest in Reno, as well as returning to the Miss Walnut Creek Festival. As he thought of the next three months his enthusiasm for the future overshadowed the ending of his high school musicals.

CHAPTER 7

I received various awards at the past three Awards Nights and won the Bank of America Award in Drama last month. I have been on the honor roll for my four years at De La Salle and presently hold a 3.6 grade point average.

The schedule he had set for himself had not been an easy one. There were times within his high school years that it seemed to him he was hopelessly behind in his studies, especially the reading assignments. Jim's opinion was that any college preparatory course work would have been demanding, but since he had set his goal to become a doctor, the additional science classes were an additional burden. If it hadn't been for his great interest in drama and music he could have handled the academic schedule more easily. He was a good student and enjoyed his studies. He remembered writing in his journal on the day he had decided to pursue a career in medicine. Although he did well in science, had a penchant to helping people and an innate desire to do something worthwhile with his life, even so, had the alternatives been equal he would have chosen a drama career.

Scanning once again the montage that his bedroom walls had become over the years, he was presented with yet another area of appreciation he had for his school. The Awards Night at the end of each year was developed to give recognition and acknowledgment to outstanding students. The certificates were a visible "well done" and encouragement to continue to achieve. The families of the men who were to be honored were invited to the annual May ceremony but had no prior knowledge as to the specific award that would be conferred. The atmosphere created was a mixture of predictable pride, anticipation and the enthusiastic congratulations of all present to the student recipients. It had seemed to Jim that the smiles of the teachers had been just as broad as those of the parents at those occasions. The teachers wanted to you succeed, challenged you to do so and gave you all the help they could. It wasn't that way at all schools. He had heard tales from kids who attended other high schools, stories of how they just "put their time in" and phrases such as, "Well, there's one teacher who cares."

Jim nodded his head, agreeing with his own thoughts, he was lucky to have been at De La Salle and he knew just what he was going to type next.

CHAPTER 8

> *As stated earlier, I'm trying for this position because I feel that I can represent the class. De La Salle has given me so much during my duration here, and you could say that I feel obliged to give it something in return. Being valedictorian would be the best way that I know to express my deep appreciation and love for this school.*

It would be a challenge to any of them appearing before the Valedictory Committee that day to express their feelings about the past four years. No guy was going to stand there and get sentimental about leaving high school. Yet Jim could express their respect and gratitude at having been part of a community of caring individuals, guided and allowed to develop their own opinions within a value system upon which they could draw the rest of their lives.

De La Salle, a private, Catholic High School, was only fifteen years old. The buildings were modern and because of vast courtyards, wide passage ways, and the liberal planting of trees gave the feeling of open space. The school had been built and was operated by the Christian Brothers who, like their lay colleagues, were proud of the fact that 90% of their graduates went on to college or university studies. Because of the large area that the school serviced, neither prospective students nor their parents could assume that application for admission would mean automatic acceptance. Jim had graduated fourth in a class of forty-four and remembered the feeling of relief when after a placement exam and a personal interview he had received a letter of acceptance.

From the very first Jim had been impressed by the friendly openness of the teachers and counselors. At the freshman orientation the class had been told that the staff was always available to them and they were. You could talk openly and freely with most of the teachers. Jim had written assignments, based on his personal opinions, that he knew would not support the Brothers' belief and had received A's. It was a graphic example that they, the students were being encouraged to think for themselves and stand for what they believed. The teachers' attitudes also served as a lesson in tolerance. Jim believed that the education the Class of 1980 had received included more than academics. They had learned how to work together yet remain individuals, worship together realizing that a man's strength can be proportionate to his faith, had fun together in the joyful expression of life and youth, and been given confidence in themselves.

As he removed the first sheet from the machine and reached for another he wondered how many would be trying out today. Mark would be there but how many others? He slipped the second sheet into the typewriter, rolled it up, indented and began to type.

CHAPTER 9

> *And, so school opened and some 170 boys, mostly strangers, appeared in the halls of De La Salle ready to start their high school education—ready for the classes, the sports, the rallies, and ready for the friendships that would obviously quickly develop.*

Friendships were very important to Jim and he had them in all ages and areas of his life. In the privacy of his room he would admit to himself that the loving, caring, sharing, with others was the most important part of life. The friends he had were friends now, but the excitement was that so many opportunities came along to meet new people and develop additional relationships. Twelve of his former classmates had entered the freshman class at De La Salle with him. It was natural that for the first few weeks they hung together. They had a common background and when you could compare reactions and the confusion of new schedules and a much larger school, it was good to have guys that you could share with, mainly because they were experiencing the same need to adjust. They had come from being the highest class in a school to—well—it seemed they had worked their way all the way to the bottom of the heap!

Jim got out of his chair and walked about the room. Why these sober thoughts? Perhaps he was pressing too hard to share his inner thoughts. He was the guy who could always keep a situation light—go for the laugh when things got tense; bring a laugh and new energy channeled toward productivity. Who was the character who did cartwheels out the main exit of "the" largest store in Walnut Creek? Why? For the heck of it! Five or six of them had been browsing through the store and the conversation had begun to lose its sparkle, there wasn't any sparkle left to the outing, and as the group was heading toward the door, not having a plan as to what to do, he looked at that broad straight runway of linoleum . . . and he cartwheeled his way out! Talk about an ice-breaker! They had laughed and carried on the rest of the afternoon.

Humor was the leveler of life, nothing could get to you as long as you could have a laugh that included you and didn't hurt anyone else. Telling jokes wasn't his brand of humor; nah, the physical was best, and a close second was writing it. Life was to be lived—his life was to be lived—enjoyed, savored and serious goals to be reached with a light heart.

Enthusiastic about his mood change, Jim crossed the room to the built-in dresser and opened the lower drawer. Under the sweaters were some papers that he had kept. Leafing through them he came across the ones he had remembers, closed the drawer and returned to his desk. Here it was, the one he had been thinking of:

THE DUCK

I knew a stupid little duck,

Who waddled all around,

In his bill he held a stick,

Which yesterday he found.

He found it by a deep blue lake,

On the sandy shore.

He looked around for other ones,

Of which there were no more.

He waddled over to a stream,

The stick still in his mouth.

And there he saw some other ducks,

But they were flying south.

He dropped the stick right where he was,

And stood right there and looked.

"I better go with them," he quacked,

Before my goose is cooked.

Smiling at his own, tongue-in-cheek, chiding, Jim refocused his attention to his speech.

CHAPTER 10

> *De La Salle has definitely given our class many opinions, attitudes and experiences; likewise, our class has given De La Salle much the same in return. As the saying goes, "You get out of something what you put into it." Well, it goes without saying that these*

people that you see before you have put in much of their spirit, knowledge, companionship to this school, and, in return, we have gotten a basis of learning.

Their high school was more than an academic program, more than the social side of passing from elementary school to college. The common characteristic the students shared, the underlying bond, was their faith. As with most ideals that the young men had, they didn't often verbalize or philosophize about their belief, yet they lived it. The respect they had and displayed for life and each other, their attained goal of maintaining De La Salle's traditions while adding their own class image and freshness, brought the realization one could be faithful to his own belief and productively function within a larger community. While attendance at most liturgical celebrations was optional, the majority of the student body attended. Jim wondered if it wasn't more powerful to display their faith in that manner rather than just sit around and talk about it.

The Religion courses, required in freshman and sophomore years and elective in junior and senior years, dealt less with doctrine and more to the clarification of the individual's values. The challenges presented by a teenage marriage. What sacrifices would have to be made? Could an individual continue his education and plan a career if he married just out of high school and had to support a wife, a family? Making a course required list of the positives and negatives of such a situation certainly was thought-provoking. Addressing one's thinking to the question of abortion, pro and con, not the opinion of your parents, the teacher, or even the church, your opinion and thought process that went into that opinion. Such exercises were preparation for adult living. Decisions have to be made daily on a large scope of lifestyle influencing situations, one not only had to have values, one had to have clearly defined in his own mind what those standards were and what situations would test them.

For Jim the open sharing on "controversial" subjects had been a new experience. Any young person knows it is easier in the long run to either keep still or agree with those around them. Especially parents, teachers and most especially institutions! Yet the teachers at De La Salle wanted his opinion—the student's thinking as well as the rationalization of that thinking. It seemed as if the forgone conclusion was that there would always be challenges, be prepared to defend your position. Without active participation from them all, without sharing your innermost thoughts openly and honestly, was to fail yourself and the class. It was an obligation that the majority of students learned to meet and the catalysis of successful learning experiences.

Jim, having opted to assume the Religion courses in his schedule the past two years, had both tempered some of his thinking and been reinforced in his attitude that individuals were to be met on just that basis. Each person had value and deserved respect. Dependent upon circumstances one's thinking could deviate from another's, yet there should be an acceptance of, a tolerance for, opinions different from his own.

Those 170 boys who had come to De La Salle four years before would be leaving with only one thing the same, they were still individuals. Better for their time together, united by time and daily activities, strengthened with the knowledge that they belonged and self-assured by reason that they were, individuals.

CHAPTER 11

We have held in our hands, strength, compassion, friendship, success, all experiences that go into making a boy a man. From becoming the freshman football Cal champs, to the outstanding and much enjoyed Sophomore Class Picnic—to the overwhelming win of the festival ticket sale, to the Junior Christmas Party, Junior Prom and Senior Breakfast, the retreats and the Senior Ball, we have displayed this strength, compassion and success, and this graduating ceremony is the physical culmination of those four years of excellence.

While the first phase of their freshman year seemed to be devoted to survival, being at the end of every line and finding their way around campus, because, or perhaps in spite of being considered the "kiddies" of the campus, sparked the class of 1980. Fresh ideas were coming and if the classes were content to ignore them they were determined to be recognized. They perceived an attitude of status quo and wanted to accomplish more. Jim was pleased that he had been involved in the student government of the school. Carrying forth the general attitude of his class had brought a new vitality to the activities his classmates were so eager to participate in. Ticket sales were a form of raising revenue for the school—their school—and as a class they were not to be denied the position of school support expressed in the highest number of sales. Upper classmen may have considered them "underlings" but they were going to leave their mark, many of them. While each boy pursued his own interests, Jim himself in the Spartan swim team and involvement in his theatrical endeavors, they were bound to the unity of being members of the class of '80. A comfortable position to be in: separate yet part of a whole. It was a chain of growth, this "whole" within a school community. Together by number of years in school, bonded by the definition of being a "class" and unified via they leadership, that they could leave a positive imprint upon the school community. True, first day of the school year in 1976, they had no plans to do much more than get through the next four years, but once complying with the identification of being a unit, a unit they became and their enthusiasm set a standard to be matched.

As they planned and executed their plans confidence and their successes encouraged them to extend themselves. Renewed school spirit was a common theme, or was it just his class explanation for wanting to do better than some who had missed an opportunity? Jim only knew that if anyone in his class was left out of an activity it was by their choice, and few chose to be left out!

There were times, depressing, sobering intervals, when some individual within the De La Salle School community died. There was talk, remembrances of encounters, identification with the man who was no longer with them. Such occasions were also a part of the growing to manhood. It seemed that when the solemnity of tragedy touched their collective lives they, not only united but, gained strength in the knowledge that there is no end, only preparation for a beginning. It was their common faith that enabled the students to experience the sorrow, happiness and the daily existence between as a way of life. Nothing to be feared, events to be shared, a greater unity than even classmates could identify to, a vulnerability that was to be acknowledged, a part of life.

Jim had anticipated a change of his life, if not death, certainly the prospect of being drafted and a possible result. He had written an assignment for his Theology class that had reflected his thinking in a number of areas. His apprehension toward the draft was common among men his age. Your plans were so indefinite when controlled by the possibility of being placed in a branch of military service. While it was just a class assignment, it was one additional avenue of thoughtful realization that his teachers had challenged him to explore. Does one cling to this existence, life, or attempt to gain an ultimate goal? A new life, a rebirth, a destination that one is encouraged to believe in from reading the Bible.

Part of life was sorrow. Jim, as most people, wasn't sure of the intrinsic relevance of this fact, yet, believed it to be fact. He and his peers had shared the grief of "Losing" one of their own. More to the support of Jim's belief; live this life to the fullest—at best it is temporary.

Yes, as a class there had been variety of experiences for each and/or all of them to meet. As individuals and a class as a whole, the challenges had been met. Their personal victories surpassed individual disappointments. They had experienced many, varied aspects of life and had, not only survived but, the courage of their convictions strengthened. Jim wanted to say "thanks," to give credit to those who had helped him and his classmates so much.

CHAPTER 12

> *I'm sure that the spirit of this class will live on at De La Salle for many years to come.*
>
> *We leave De La Salle to continue on with our lives, but all leave with a great spirit and self-confidence that one acquires from participating in such a school as this. Some of us will take that spirit to colleges and universities—others will take it to jobs that await them, but whatever our future quests may be, we will know that within ourselves we carry the spirit and tradition of De La Salle.*

As an incoming freshman four years seemed a very long time. Retrospectively from this bright May morning four years had passed very quickly. Too quickly in some ways. Now there were friends to say goodbye to, activities he would no longer be involved in, familiar surroundings that he would no longer frequent. Already the customary promises of not to lose track of one another were being verbalized. Yet each knew their relationships would never be exactly the same. They would grow in different interests, have less in common as to daily activities. They could have times when they would talk about differences in their lives, but they would no longer have shared the same experiences. Jim rose from the chair, took the third page of his speech from the typewriter and carried it with him to the window. As he looked down into the yard he could visualize a poster he had seen recently. The poster had a picture of a boat at anchor. The caption read, "A ship is safe in the protection of a harbor. But is that what a ship is constructed for?" At least that is how he remembered it. He tried to imagine himself as a ship— docked in a harbor, waiting to be set a sail on risky seas. It seemed an apt description of his feelings. He wanted to sail—to take risks—to accomplish what he had been "built" for. He had always kept busy; this was his choice, he not only felt better physically when he was active but mentally. There was so much to savor in life and he wanted to get all of it in. In the past year his zest for experiencing life and all of its activities had become, compulsive, it seemed even to him that he had to make the choices he had made. Yes, he was over extending himself in many instances; he was driven by—by what? He wasn't sure, a sense of awareness, that if he didn't take advantage of the opportunities presented you might not get another chance to take part in the vibrancy of life. On February 22, 1980 he had written a "Dialogue with Body":

> *Look Jim, you know what you've been putting me through the past couple weeks? This musical is driving me crazy.*
>
> *Sorry! But wait till you go through the coming weeks. I sure hope that you can "stomach it."*
>
> *Ha! Ha!*
>
> *Just try to give me a little rest.*
>
> *I see that I'm going to have to get you in shape.*
>
> *Fine, but for now, let's just take it easy so I can recuperate.*

Jim gathered the three page speech and slipped it in the binder he would take with him to school. He went to the closet, opened the door and pulled what he would wear that day. He continued to think about the people who kept telling him to slow down, parents, friends, "Don't take on so much Jim," "Jim you are too tired," . . . they simply did not realize, they were well intentioned, but they didn't share his belief that you only had one chance and you had better do everything you wanted to do before it was too late.

He had his job at the bank for the summer, he and his buddy had their apartment for next year, he made himself the same promise for his college years that he had made for high school; he would be involved. UCLA, all it had to offer, a career in medicine, certainly he would marry and have a family. Jim had always wanted to father twins—why? What goes into making a dream? He just wanted his family to have a set of twins, maybe two . . .

Laughing at himself he realized he had to first grab a shower, get to school, tryout for valedictorian, enjoy the post graduation parties, surpass his own performance standards of excellence at both the Miss Nevada and Miss Walnut Creek ceremonies and continue to give thanks for his joy of life.

As he gathered the things he wanted to take to the shower he remembered the "Thanksgiving" poem he had written last year, snatches of it anyway. Love of people, appreciation of the gift of life, if Jim chose to be a ship, his sails were full and he was eager for each breeze that would move him to his potential. Yep, he was thankful for all he had had and for all that could come.

As he reached to open his bedroom door he heard sounds indicating that the rest of the family was beginning the day. If it happened that he would win the valedictorian position, wouldn't they be in for a surprise. Valediction, to say farewell. He wanted to make this transition in his life a time to remember. To publicly acknowledge the gratitude he felt, bring awareness of his appreciation to those who were supportive of his efforts . . . thanks and farewell to eighteen years of—"what went into making a boy a man."

PROLOGUE

This is the last written remembrance there was in Jim's room, his valedictorian speech. Jim gave this speech only once and it was not at his graduation exercises. The friend who had encouraged Jim to express his ideas and thoughts was chosen to be valedictorian of the class.

Academically Jim graduated twelfth in his class and it was not until after the ceremonies that he shared his hopes of being chosen as valedictorian with his family. He completed his commitment to his summer job, received the wholehearted approval of the audiences of both the Miss Nevada and Miss Walnut Creek Pageant, and regardless of his humility, heard the applause and relished in the feeling of being admired and loved by both strangers and friends.

Meticulously Jim said his goodbyes, expressed his thanks, one to one and in a manner that the recipients described as "not like Jim." What his reason was, making sure that he had acknowledged that which he harbored in his heart; he poignantly bade his farewell to the people who had brought joy to his life. College would bring a new beginning, a new start . . . it seemed as if he wanted all to be aware that he did indeed appreciate and love them.

Jim Malan died in a single car accident on August 24, 1980. Returning home from a post-party celebration of the Miss Walnut Creek Pageant, his car was found by a newspaper truck driver, the car, Jim's car, was wedged into a tree.

As with any tragic loss, speculations were rampant as the news of Jim's death spread through the small community. "I told him to slow down!" There were those who, after hearing the account of his death, wondered if he had "partied" too much? Was he drunk? Was Jim too tired, did he fall asleep at the wheel of his car?

It is known that Jim was not under the influence of alcohol or any other self-induced substance that could have caused his varying from his established record of competent driving. Was the accident caused by fatigue? While through speculation, anything is possible, it seems unlikely that Jim, a performer accustomed to pacing his energy, would be unaware of the level of fatigue he might have been experiencing.

Did Jim have a "premonition" of his death? Is this an explanation to the fact that he was more demonstrative in his "thank you" and "goodbyes?" We humans have a tendency to want every question to have an answer, each preponderance to be satisfied by the ultimate answer. Yet we accept the fact that there are times that we will have no answer. We must live only with the knowledge of, faith in, another human being, a friend. To those who believe that Jim believed his life would be short, they can be content that he lived it well, genuinely cared for those with whom he came in contact with, and exemplified the fact that he was never too rushed to display his regard for others.

Jim Malan was not too different from his friends. Perhaps he displayed his talents when others would not have the courage to attempt to do so. Maybe the fact that he would risk to run for student government offices showed the courage of his convictions; he had an underlying desire to be not just part of his society, but to bring life, laughter and a reason for being to it, to himself. To be passive was not in Jim's nature. He shared his gifts of talents, humor, education and belief that each of us is on this earth to be, to help, and look out for each other. He expressed it better than many and that is what made him "special" to those who knew him.

On stage or off, Jim did not consider himself a "star." Others elevated him to that position. He had a captivating quality in his personality; even in the most superficial of encounters people he interacted with were lighter of heart because of the encounter. Those around him made Jim a "star," not just for his performances in theatrical endeavors, but because of his basic concern for others, and because he was what many wanted to be: bright, attractive, accepted and loved.

Eighteen years is not a long time to be alive. How much can one person accomplish in eighteen years? Well those who had even the briefest of a meeting with Jim Malan are aware that even a moment when someone cares that you are alive is long enough. Jim was that spark, that tangible quality that allowed you to think well of yourself.

Eighteen years, or eighteen years multiplied by 10's of years, Jim was a bit of magic that touched many lives. His music, song renditions, acting, work for and within his church, loyalty and honesty with all; we each are capable of recognizing a good person within moments of meeting them. He had the ability to be "one of the guys," enjoy the partying and the pranks—he was many things to many people. And so aren't we all?

***

Seton Award Nomination

The first annual Seton Awards will be presented by the Oakland Diocesan Department of Education to those persons who best typify the spirit of the Catholic school in its traditions of proclaiming the Word; building community and/or rendering service.

We particularly wish to discover and honor those persons who quietly, day by day, love and pursue these traditions.

The award is named for Mother Elizabeth Seton, wife, mother and foundress of a religious order who was canonized in 1975. She is the first American born saint of the Catholic Church.

Elizabeth Seton, born into a wealthy and distinguished New York Episcopalian family, could scarcely have predicted the turn of events which would lead to her canonization as a saint of the Roman Catholic Church 200 years later.

Severe reverses of fortune, the sickness and death of her husband, left her an impoverished widow with five small children to support.

Rejection by friends and relatives when she converted to Catholicism, led her to Emmetsburg, Maryland where she opened the first Catholic school in the United States. From this tiny seed was to come the foundation of the American Sisters of Charity, a community which blazed the trail for the Catholic parochial school system and uncounted other works of Catholic social service. Elizabeth Seton was characterized by her strong faith which she imparted to others through her teaching, example and service.

The only requirement of nomination for the Seton award is that the nominee be a graduate of a Catholic elementary or high school located in the Diocese of Oakland (Alameda and Contra Costa counties).

Any individual or group is eligible to nominate. Self nominations are also acceptable.

Nominations will be reviewed by a screening committee. Final selections will be made by a panel of distinguished judges.

To be considered, nominations must be received by January 15, 1981.

Nomination for is attached. More nomination blanks may be obtained from the Diocese Department of Education, 2900 Lakeshore Avenue, Oakland, CA 94610, or call 893-4711.

Letter submitted with nomination form by Mrs. P.T. Barlow

The name of JIM MALAN is respectively submitted for consideration of the Seton Award. Jim's life, in the prideful estimation of his many friends, typifies the spirit of Catholic education; courage of conviction, proclaiming the Word via life style, effective in building community and his sharing of God given talents.

Jimmy, the eldest of the three children, attended St. Isidore School in Danville. Memories of the slight framed youngster with the broad smile and outgoing personality remain with his grade school teachers. Maintaining high academic grades never limited the time Jimmy gave to establishing friendships or involvement in family projects and extracurricular activities. Scouting, newspaper routes, swim teams, music lessons, helping around home and babysitting were all part of Jim's out of school hours. His participation on the school Track and Field Team did not hamper him from winning the school Poetry Contest three consecutive years, receiving awards in Spanish, Literature, Music and first place in the Ballroom Dance Contest. Jim was the first student selected to be a lector at St. Isidore's. Playing the organ during Mass was Jim's special gift to both God and parishioners, a talent he would later share with members of St. Anne's parish near the Rossmoor Retirement Community. He was also a member of his parish Folk Group, having taught himself to play the guitar. Regardless of age, everyone seemed just a bit lighter of heart for having been with Jim. When he graduated from St. Isidore's School he left with the love, hopes and respect of classmates and staff members alike.

While a student at De La Salle High School, Jim continued his joyful appreciation of life and of those around him. Achieving the honor roll all four years did not deter him from being actively involved on the school newspaper, a member of the Liturgy Planning Committee, participating on the Spartan Swim Team, Sophomore Class President, Rally Club, Student Council member in his junior year and a member of the De La Salle-Carondelet High School Mixed Chorus. Jim not only participated in these organizations and activities but excelled in them . . . swimming trophies, leads in musical productions, recipient of the Drama Award presented by the Bank of America and was presented a lifetime membership in the Thespian Club.

Summers and school breaks would find Jim establishing his own swimming school. His natural rapport with people could be exemplified by the success of his swimming students, some of whom had attended long established swim schools, yet had not overcome their fear of the water until they came under Jim's instruction. Part-time employment in sales and as a clerk at the Walnut Creek Branch of Bank of America indicate both the diversification of Jim's ability and his initiative.

While Jim's theatrical credits include the Willows Youth Theatre productions, an entertainer at the Miss Nevada Contest of 1980, Young People's Productions of the Walnut Creek Civic Arts

Theatre, an appearance on the Romper Room television show, an entertainer at the Miss Walnut Creek Pageant for four years, his innate humility remained intact. Jim shared, always, his successes with his fellow performers.

Graduated with double honors and receiving the Physiology Aware from De La Salle High School in June 1980, Jim had been educated in, grew within, and lived his faith. Reflecting on his four years at De La Salle, Jim expressed his appreciation of his Catholic education when he wrote, "We have held in our hands, strength, compassion friendship, success, all experiences that go into making a boy a man . . ."

Accepted as a pre-med student by UCLA, Jim's choice of studies, once again, reflected his deep desire to help people and his inexhaustible ability to share.

For the first time in twelve years, JIM MALAN will be unable to share his talent in the celebration of Catholic Schools Week. This outstanding young man, a nominee for the Seton Award, was killed in a single car accident in August 1980.

Remembrances – Jim's Last Days

By Barbara Malan

Jim's first night on stage in high school he played the part of "Wally Webb." He was a young 12-year-old who dies of appendicitis in the play. Jim was a freshman. Jim's last night of his life, he was the dead boy.

Jim's hit song in "Guys and Dolls" was "Sit Down, You're Rockin' the Boat." It was about sinking on a boat and going to heaven.

Jim bought a "Heaven" shirt, summer of 1980. It had a picture of "lying on a grave" at Treasure Island in Disneyland – <u>for fun?</u>

Co', Kelly and Ginny all woke up at 4:00 a.m. Sunday morning the 25th. Denise woke up at 4:00 a.m. also, screaming that she was dying. Her grandmother had to wake her up. Carla's hair, which was always straight, kept curly for the following weeks after the show.

Jim kept saying he had to get it all in – his fun, shows, beach, etc.

Jack told Jim his personal info regarding his adoption two weeks prior.

At Cindy's home (post pageant party) when he was leaving he said to his family, NaNa, PopPop, no more curfews. I have no time to be home. It is my life. It is my last night with my friends and I will be home later.

At Joe's home, Jim told his friends how happy he was that we adopted him.

At Cindy's reception party NaNa told him she had been to his first show in Radio City ten years ago and tonight you are the star. NaNa, PopPop begged him to stop and sleep at their home rather than drive to Danville. Their home in Walnut Creek was not far from the reception. He declined and said he had to get home. It was Dad's birthday and he had to cut the lawn for the family celebration on Sunday.

He also was to play the organ at St. Anne's Church in Walnut Creek for his last time Sunday morning.

Diane dreamed Jim died that night.

Jim finished his last stage performance the night of the 24th.

Jim wore a red rose that evening on his tux lapel after the show and would not take it off.

After his Walnut Creek pageant that evening, Jim kissed and hugged Patti (his teacher/director of the plays, musicals, dances, etc. for all of his four years at De La Salle) and told her, "Goodbye and thank you."

ABOOKS

ALIVE Book Publishing and ALIVE Publishing Group
are imprints of Advanced Publishing LLC,
3200 A Danville Blvd., Suite 204, Alamo, California 94507

Telephone: 925.837.7303
alivebookpublishing.com

www.ingramcontent.com/pod-product-compliance
Lightning Source LLC
Chambersburg PA
CBHW060940170426
43195CB00025B/2988